RAILWAYS OF NORTH WALES

THE
LLANGOLLEN
LINE
RUABON TO BARMOUTH

Ruabon 1957

Photo: J.W.T. House courtesy C.L. Caddy

COMPILED and WRITTEN BY

BILL REAR & NORMAN JONES

With additional material by D. J. Lowe

First Published by Foxline Publishing 1990
This Edition Published by Book Law Publications 2012

Printed by The Amadeus Press, Cleckheaton, BD19 4TQ

ACKNOWLEDGEMENTS

We wish to thank the following for their photographic contribution:- Peter E. Baughan, G. Biddle, for his own work and the collection of R.E.G. Read, C.L. Caddy for his own work, and the collection of the late Joe House, with grateful thanks to Mrs. M. House, W.A. Camwell, Clwyd Record Office, the late Derek Cross, A. Donaldson, R.W. Hinton, John Keylock, Norman Kneale, the late T. Lewis, J.H. Moss, the Welsh Industrial and Maritime Museum - Dr. Stuart Owen Jones, Mrs. K.M. Platt and Mrs Carole Swainston for access to their late husbands' collections, Speed Publications and M. Welch. We also wish to thank the following for their contibution:- John Roberts of Rhyd Uchaf, Bala, former signalman at Llanuwchllyn, Driver Roy Sharrock, Fireman J.A.Jones and Inspector F.W.Wiggett formerly of Chester M.P.D., Vic. Roberts and Bob Dennis of B.R. Chester, Frank Parish of Bala Lake Railway, and Colin Jones of Cwm Penmachno, Henry Wilson of Tarvin, G.Haulfryn Williams and Gwynedd Archives, D.Southern of Llangollen Railway, T.Roberts of Johnstown P.O. and former driver at Croes Newydd M.P.D., Rowland Pittard of Bridgend & Derek Foster of Kirkby, Liverpool. Especial thanks to John Kimberley for all the invaluable help and assistance in the preparation of this work.

2. Bala Junction. 1937,
Photo: G.H.Platt.

THE LLANGOLLEN LINE, RUABON TO BARMOUTH

HISTORICAL

The 54.5 miles from Ruabon to Barmouth through the Dee valley was the epitome of a GWR secondary main line in rural Wales. The route had its origins in various proposals dating from 1847, when a scheme was proposed for a line from Birkenhead to Llangollen, with a branch from the Shrewsbury and Chester Railway. Due to the economic state of the country following the depression which succeeded the railway mania, nothing more surfaced to provide the vale of Llangollen with railway facilities, until November 1853 when a scheme materialised to link Ruabon and Rhyl, followed in the next year with a proposal to link Cefn, on the S.& C. with a line referred to as The Llangollen Railway. This was supported by the London & North Western Railway, but rejected in favour of the Vale of Llangollen Railway backed by the GWR and which received the Royal Assent on 1st August 1859. Construction was by Thomas Brassey. The line left the Shrewsbury & Chester just south of Ruabon, and was laid as a single line with provision for doubling, this incorporated in the formation. Intermediate stations were constructed at Acrefair and Trevor where a connection was made with the canal basin. The line opened to freight traffic on 1st December 1861 and to passengers on 2nd June 1862. From the start it was worked by the GWR.

The Llangollen to Corwen Railway was incorporated by Act of 6th August 1860, the GWR having prepared the plans for the extension in 1859 as part of a scheme to reach the Cambrian coast. The line followed the course of the River Dee but the construction was hampered by the terrain and tunneling was necessary at Berwyn. Nevertheless by 1865 the line had been inspected by Captain Rich and passed as suitable for traffic which commenced on 8th May 1865. Connection with the Vale of Llangollen line was by end-on junction, and so a new station was built at Llangollen on the site of the present station. Connection was made with the Denbigh, Ruthin & Corwen Railway which arrived at the latter town on 6th October 1864 using a temporary structure until the permanent station was opened to traffic on 11th October 1865, which served both the D.R.& C. and the line from Ruabon.

By October 1860 a number of projects linking Corwen and Bala were in the air. There was a "Corwen, Bala and Barmouth Railway" which proposed connecting the Denbigh, Ruthin and Corwen Railway with the Aberystwith and Welch Coast railway (sic). The GWR had designs on taking over the D.R.& C.R. and the Vale of Clwyd line, whilst a further proposal was the "West Midland, Shrewsbury and Coast of Wales". Details of these schemes can be found in Peter Baughans work A Regional History of the Railways of Great Britain, Volume 11

3. Ruabon Cefn Junction. 5th July 1952. The lowered signal gives No.**6316** and its train for Barmouth a clear road for the Llangollen line. The two lamps on the bufferbeam indicate this is a Class A train. Ruabon South signal box, sitting on the embankment to the right by the rear of the train replaced an earlier box on the opposite side of the line.
Photo: T.Lewis.

- North and Mid Wales. Suffice to say that they were all unsuccessful. By 1862 modified proposals were examined by a Parliamentary Committee and two schemes which ultimately provided the through route materialised. These were the Corwen & Bala Railway, and the Bala to Dolgelly. From the latter place, an end on junction with the Aberystwith & Welch Coast Railway at Barmouth Junction was effected. The Act of 21st July 1863 provided for a joint station at Dolgellau.

By 1866 the line from Corwen to Llandrillo was opened for traffic with the remaining section finally commencing operations on 1st April 1868. Meanwhile, construction of the Bala to Dolgelly Railway had proceeded and by July 1868 had survived a visit by the Inspectorate who approved the work and the line, business commencing on 4th August 1868. Nevertheless, there was some delay at Dolgellau where the Cambrian Railway (successors to the A.& W.C.R.) experienced difficulties which were eventually resolved.

From the outset the GWR had worked the line and until the Cambrian Railway was absorbed by the GWR in 1922 the latter were denied access to the Cardigan Bay coast. This presented the unusual and unique situation at Dolgellau where there were two separate stations on the same site with their respective Station Masters and their offices facing one another across the tracks. The situation was rationalised with amalgamation and the two buildings on their respective platforms remained until closure and demolition. The GWR absorbed the Bala and Dolgelly line in 1877 but did not amalgamate with the Corwen & Bala, the Llangollen & Corwen and the Vale of Llangollen lines until 1896. Quite naturally, traffic developed and improvements were made from time to time. In 1877 a second platform and passing loop was installed at Glyndyfrdwy. A connection was made at Bala in 1880 with the Bala to Ffestiniog branch, with Bala Town station being opened on 1st November 1882. The original Bala station closed when a new station called Bala Junction which provided interchange facilities for passengers, opened. Bala Junction never appeared in public timetables and had no road access. The former terminus subsequently reopened as Bala Lake Halt.

In 1900 the line between Ruabon and Llangollen was doubled and Pentrefelin sidings west of Llangollen station were extended to provide additional storage for carriages and wagons. At the same time, Acrefair, Trevor and Llangollen stations were remodelled. In 1905 Sun Bank Halt was brought into use. During W.W.I., passing loops were installed at Deeside, between Berwyn and Glyndyfrdwy, and at Garneddwen. In 1920s Bontnewydd was reconstructed with a new loop and platforms west of the original station, and in the 1930s halts were opened at Bonwm, Llangower, Llys, Garneddwen, Wnion and Dolserau. Sun Bank Halt and Dolserau did not remain open for long after 1945, but the remaining halts survived until the closure of the line.

The proposal to link Bala with Ffestiniog was made originally by the Vale of Llangollen Railway, described in the promotion as the Bala, Festiniog and Penrhyndeudraeth Railway. The Bill was withdrawn but a new proposal surfaced in 1873 when the GWR backed a new company, the Bala & Festiniog

under an Act of 28th July 1873. Capital was raised by the GWR, the Vale of Llangollen, the Llangollen & Corwen and the Corwen & Bala lines. The line commenced at Llangower (Bala Junction) to the Festiniog & Blaenau Railway station at Ffestiniog. The F.& B. was to be acquired and converted to standard gauge. This Company and the Bala & Festiniog lines were subsequently purchased, confirmed by the GWR Act of 1880.

The line to Festiniog was opened on 1st November 1882 although the re-gauged F.& B. line was not inspected for running until July 1883. Due to the stations at Manod and Blaenau not being complete, opening was delayed until a further inspection on 3rd August 1883 passed the line as satisfactory. The F.& B. section re-opened on 10th September 1883. Stations were initially provided at Bala Town, Frongoch, Arenig, Trawsfynydd, Maentwrog Road and Festiniog. In 1902 a station was provided at Cwm Prysor, whilst Trawsfynydd was extended and modified in 1911 with two special platforms for military use. Halts were erected at Tyddyn Bridge, Capel Celyn, Bryncelynog, Llafar and Trawsfynydd Lake. Between Ffestiniog and Blaenau there was one station at Manod until after WW1 when Teigl Halt was opened.

TRAFFIC

Traffic between Ruabon and Barmouth Junction was sparse, although in the early years there was an optimism that much would be generated. The line suffered from the fact that the countryside was thinly populated, and apart from the industrial belt between Llangollen and Ruabon there was not much likelihood of any development which would be of great benefit. The centres of population were contained at Llangollen, Corwen, Bala and Dolgellau and although intermediate halts were provided, generally there was just enough traffic to cover costs. Prior to the First World War the railway had a monopoly and could dictate conditions. Examination of the station returns show a steady decline after the war against rising costs, mainly due to wages. For example at Berwyn in 1913 the annual wages bill was £69 whilst total receipts for the year were £446. By 1923

4. Ruabon. 19th July 1963. The British Railways Standard Class 4MT 4-6-0 locomotives had taken over many duties from former G.W.R. locomotives with the transfer of lines north of Wolverhampton from the Western Region to the L.M. and the through trains from Barmouth to Chester were increasingly worked by these engines, Here **75020**, working the 2/35pm from Barmouth to Chester pulls away from north end of Ruabon past the water column and under the minor road bridge on the short run to Wrexham.The first coach is L.M.R. stock.   *Photo: Peter E.Baughan.*

wages had risen to £169 against receipts of £677 and by 1935 the wages were £168 and receipts £370. In 1903 there were 2 staff employed at the station but by 1913 this had been halved and so remained until the last figure available (1935) when returns listed 1 member on the staff.

In 1903 **Llangollen** had a staff total of 20 with a wages bill of £1027 against total receipts of £13852. Receipts had risen by 1923 to £19258 with 16 staff, but dwindled to £8920 by 1935 with 13 staff. In that year 19519 passenger tickets were issued and total freight goods tonnage for the same year amounted to 7743 against a peak of 19847 in 1903.

Corwen returned similar figures. In 1903 there were 33 staff employed with a wage bill of £2333 p.a. and total receipts of £8878. 42444 tickets were issued and 12140 tons of freight traffic handled. Peak year was 1923 when 28 staff had a wages bill of £5162 and total traffic receipts amounted to £14522. 43427 passenger tickets were issued in that year although the peak figure of 76163 tickets had been issued in 1913. Freight traffic was marginally up 13879 tons against a peak in 1913 of 20758 tons. By 1935, 22 staff drew £4014 per annum with total receipts of £9879. 22119 passenger tickets were issued in that year and total freight tonnage amounted to 11269.

Bala station had 18 staff in 1903 with an annual wages bill of £999 and total receipts of £8797, freight tonnage being 10365. By 1923, the peak year, 20 staff drew £3162 p.a. in wages with total receipts of £13421. 39379 passenger tickets were issued and freight tonnage amounted to 10007 which was the lowest figure until 1933 and 1934. By 1935, 25 staff drew £3918 p.a. in wages. It is believed that the increase in staff was due to the expansion of the Locomotive Department which took some staff from Corwen which had closed by 1929. Receipts for 1935 were £8312 which showed a decline from its peak year of 1931 when receipts then totalled £12146. A total of 26593 tickets were issued and freight tonnage was 13349, below the peak year of 1931 when 21457 tons were dealt with. Bala station returns included Bala Junction and Bala Lake Halt. Because Bala Station Master was located on the Ffestiniog branch its returns were not included in the Ruabon to Barmouth line figures.

Dolgelly's returns cannot be compared before the 1923

figures, due to the fact that the figures only refer to the GWR receipts. In that year 17 staff drew £2338 p.a. against total receipts of £18512. Some 44296 passenger tickets were issued and freight tonnage amounted to 11254. Peak year was 1929 when 18 staff drew £2780 against receipts of £19057. 35858 tickets were issued and 13490 tons of freight were handled. By 1935 the figures were as follows:

19 staff drew £2834 p.a. Total receipts amounted to £15673. 37673 passenger tickets were issued and freight tonnage had dropped from 18087 tons the previous year to 14618 tons.

These line totals give some idea of the profitability of the route. Peak year was 1923 when 112 staff drew £16555 p.a. in wages. Total receipts for the line amounted to £109622. 348411 passenger tickets were issued and 140990 tons of freight handled. Freight tonnage peaked in 1929 at 151629 tons and fell drastically in 1931, followed by an increase in successive years. By 1935, 102 staff were employed drawing £15261 p.a., Total receipts were £78880, showing a decline again after reaching £82083 the previous year. Ticket sales nevertheless were up by 12917 on the previous year at 179848. Total freight tonnage was also up to 132027, increasing annually from 1930.

On the Ffestiniog branch, returns for Bala have already been given. The most profitable station on the line was Trawsfynydd, with 1923 providing the peak year. 5 staff drew £908 p.a. wages but this excluded the Motive Power Department. Total traffic receipts were £19264. 37267 tickets were issued (peak year of 1903 issued 55211). Freight tonnage amounted in 1923 to 4107 (bettered in 1930 [4982], 1935 [4916].

TIME TABLES

The earliest working time table to hand is the G.W.R. Service book for **May 1907**, listed as Section 13 and covering the Chester district. In common with all GWR Time Table issues the Service books showed both passenger and freight workings and apart from district boundary revisions remained similar in presentation and uniform in style until the issue dated 20th.September 1954, when some sections changed to the British Railways standard format. However, the Chester and Central Wales Districts retained the GWR format until the issue dated 19th.September 1955.

In 1907, the section from Ruabon (Llangollen Line Junction box) to Corwen West remained open continuously apart from Sundays 5.30am to 5/30pm, although Trevor and Carrog boxes were switched out daily. A class K goods train left Ruabon yard at 12.45am, Mondays Excepted, for Corwen, running non stop to Glyndyfrdwy where it waited twenty minutes before continuing, arriving at Corwen at 2.10am. The first through working to Dolgellau was a class F freight which left Ruabon yard at 4.20am and called briefly at Llangollen passenger station for 3 minutes, then ran non stop to Corwen where it waited another 13 minutes, then on to Bala Junction where it halted for eight minutes. The train stopped to pin down brakes at the gradient board at Garneddwen and arrived at Dolgellau at 6.25am., The first Down passenger left Ruabon at 7.50am, called at all stations and arrived at Dolgellau

6. Sun Bank Halt. c.1956. Running tender first, a 43XX Class 2-6-0 ushers a five coach Ruabon to Barmouth train, (See 'Coach Workings') past the site of Sun Bank Halt, coaled to its tender's 6 ton capacity. The photographer has crossed the line from the previous view and faced east. Life-expired sleepers lie in the cess awaiting removal, those (centre left) placed transversely awaiting the next engineer's line occupation. Observe also the replacement rails aligned in the 'four foot'. *Photo: C.L.Caddy.*

7. Bala Junction. 31st May 1963. A westward facing view at Bala Junction as B.R. Standard 4MT 4-6-0 No.**75021** leaves with the two coach 7.17am ex Ruabon. To the right an 0-6-0PT hurries away with the single coach shuttle to Bala (Town.) Of note in the centre foreground is the early form of lamp-post and 'half-harp' suspension bracket. Also of interest are the two purpose-built single-pitch roof per-way 'bothies', one extreme left, the other near the Bala train. The code of 'audible' signalling engine whistles or 'crows' were used at the Junction pre-scribed as follows: DOWN TRAINS. To Dolgelley, Down Platform - 2 whistles, To Dolgelley, from Festiniog Loop, 6, To Bala Station, 3, To Siding, 4, UP TRAINS. From Bala Station - 3 whistles, From Dolgelley to Up plat-form, 1, From Dolgelley, to Festiniog Loop, 6, From Siding, 4.
Photo: Peter E. Baughan.

8. Bala. 10th June 1952. 43XX Class 2-6-0 No.**7305** (84J Croes Newydd,) with a Class K freight for Ruabon. The wagon checker attends to the labelling, *Rule No.117 'Cattle - conveyance of,'* being inapplicable, as the leading vehicle contains no bovine passengers. Stout bars bracing buffer beam to smoke-box, combined with outside steam pipes, give the class a distinctive and puissant aspect. Between the leading wheels is the Automatic Train Control apparatus, note its robust construction. The low-slung magnetic inductor shoe was fitted to precise limits to be within the magnetic field of the fixed ramp in the 'four-foot'. The system, installed by the G.W.R. in the decade ending 1939 gave audible cab-signals, a bell for a "clear" distant signal, a hooter at "caution. An automatic brake application took place if the driver did not respond. For technical reasons applicable to single-line working the system was not operable on the Ruabon-Barmouth route.
Photo: W.G.Rear.

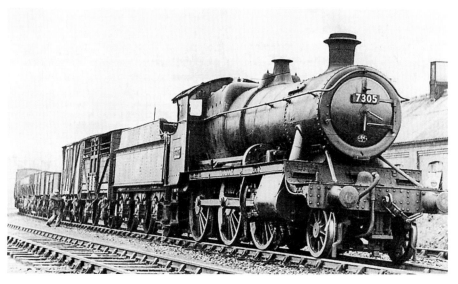

at 9.45am. There were 5 passenger through trains in the Down direction with a motor train working between Ruabon and Llangollen, (5 trips), between Ruabon and Corwen (3 trips), Ruabon and Bala (1 trip), and Ruabon and Llanuwchllyn (1 trip). In addition to the freight turns mentioned, there were additional workings over various sections of the line but no through freight workings in the Down direction. On a Sunday there were two freight workings, the 12.45am Ruabon to Corwen and the 4.20am Ruabon to Dolgellau with two motor train workings between Ruabon and Corwen.

In the Up direction, the first train of the day departed Corwen at 2.20am (MX) for Ruabon, stopping at the gradient board at Acrefair to pin down brakes, and arrived Ruabon yard at 3.15am. There were four passenger workings between Dolgellau and Ruabon, the last through working of the day being the Mail train which departed from Dolgellau at 7/35pm and arrived at Ruabon at 9/42pm. There were no through goods workings, but there were three goods departures daily from Dolgellau to Corwen. Most of the duties were worked by Corwen locomotive department.

With the amalgamation in the early twenties, the Divisional structure of the G.W.R. changed to accommodate the extra Districts and consequently Chester Division became Area 14 and which until 1937 included the former Cambrian Railways territory. By 1935 the signal boxes along the line closed down for the night and freight trains were reduced in number. The first Down train of the day departed Ruabon at 4.03am, arriving at Barmouth at 6.56am. and calling at all stations but not the halts. It was entitled Mail and Goods, and ran as a class F working. A through freight class K departed Ruabon at 4.45am, arriving at Barmouth Junction at 8.33am. Other freight workings ran over part of the line only, but through working

BRITISH RAILWAYS
WESTERN REGION

SERVICE TIME TABLES

CHESTER, BIRKENHEAD, MANCHESTER AND WOLVERHAMPTON

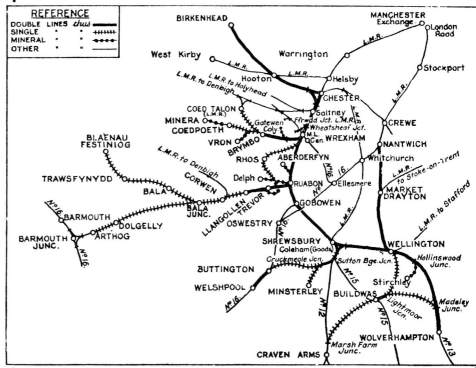

REFERENCE
DOUBLE LINES *thus* ———
SINGLE " " ++++++
MINERAL " " ◄◄◄◄
OTHER " "

SEPTEMBER 26th, 1949
until further notice

IMPORTANT NOTICE.

The time specified in the Time Tables is the departure from the station when the times of arrival and departure are not stated, and in such cases the trains should ARRIVE in sufficient time to enable the work to be done in order to leave the station at the time appointed.

The advertised departure times in a number of instances are slightly earlier than the Service Book times and the former must be used in all quotations to the public. The trains must also leave at the ADVERTISED time whenever practicable.

FOR POINT-TO-POINT RUNNING TIMES FOR THROUGH EXPRESS PASSENGER TRAINS, SEE PAGE 5.

of wagons was accomplished without undue loss of time. The first through passenger working was the 7.20am from Wrexham calling all stations and halts except Sun Bank Halt and arrived at Barmouth at 10.10am. The next through working departed Ruabon at 9.36am (from Birkenhead), 12/46pm (from Wrexham); 1/17pm FSX,1/30pmFSO; 3/05pm; 5/10pm (SO); and 6/35pm (from Birkenhead) arriving Barmouth at 9/05pm. In addition there were several passenger workings to Llangollen, Cor-

wen and Bala some working as Auto trains, in one case running from Chester to Corwen (dep Chester 1/15pm, Ruabon 1/58pm and Corwen arr. 2/39pm). There was one through working on a Sunday, dep. Ruabon 11.10am arrive Barmouth 1/08pm, which returned from there at 7/15pm arrive Ruabon 9/16pm. There were three local journeys between Ruabon and Llangollen in the afternoon in each direction, and a through working from Liverpool Lime St. to Llangollen, arriving at 3/12pm. It departed from

Llangollen for Lime Street at 7/35pm. In the Up direction, the first through departure left Barmouth at 7.40am calling most stations and halts and arrived at Ruabon at 10.00am. There was one through freight train from Barmouth Junction during the week and two on a Saturday, both in the early evening, the daily train departing 8/00pm arriving Ruabon at 12.11am and was the last through train of the day. The Saturdays Only train left Barmouth Junction at 5/25pm and arrived Ruabon at 11/12pm. There were 5 through passenger workings, including the 7.40am, Saturdays excepted, and eight through workings on a Saturday. These generally worked to Wrexham although the 10.15am and the 2/35pm worked to Birkenhead.

In 1937 the Central Wales lines were abstracted from the Chester district and created as a new Division with Offices at Oswestry. This was given Section 16 reference.

The wartime issue for **May 1941** covers passenger trains only, and shows five trains daily in the Down direction, including the 4.33am Mails and Goods. In addition there were five trips from Ruabon to Llangollen, or Bala during the day. However there were only four through trains in the Up direction, of which one ran through to Birkenhead, and the 7/15pm from Barmouth (Mails) ran through to Chester. There were also five workings from Bala or Llangollen.

The freight time table for **October 1942** also lists the 4.33am Mails to Barmouth followed by the through goods 12 minutes later. The latter arrived at Barmouth at 9.04am, one hour and twenty one minutes after the Mails. There was one other through freight to Barmouth Junction which departed Ruabon 7.50am and arrived at its destination at 5/05pm, taking eight hours and fifteen minutes for the 52 miles. There were three trips to Bala daily although two were listed as RR [**R**uns as **R**equired]. There were three trips from Ruabon to Trevor Goods Sidings, again one was RR and one was SX. In the Up direction The two through workings departed Barmouth Junction at 11.06am arrive Ruabon at 6/48pm; and 7/00pm arrive Ruabon at 12.01am. There was a conditional freight starting from Dolgelley at 5.55am to Ruabon, due 11.47am. and no less than five trips from Bala to Ruabon of which two were RR and one of these SX.

The last summer issue prior to nationalization dated **June 1947** showed that not much had changed after the war. The 4.33am Mails still ran in the same times as did the 4.45am goods. There were still only six through trains daily SX, although some now ran beyond Barmouth to Pwllheli. There were nine through trains on a Saturday of which one was the Mail and four worked through to Pwllheli. A freight left Ruabon for Barmouth junction at 7.50am daily arriving there at 4/21pm, and other freight trains ran from Ruabon to Blaenau Ffestiniog, Bala and Llangollen. Auto trains continued to run between Ruabon and Llangollen, Corwen and Bala in some cases working from Wrexham. The auto working from Chester had disappeared. There were no Sunday workings shown. In the Up direction the first train from Dolgellau was the 5.45am freight to Ruabon, preceded from Bala by a train for Birkenhead. The first departure from Barmouth left at 7.18am for Ruabon. There were five through passenger workings to Ruabon or beyond SX. with eight through workings on Saturdays including two to Birmingham Snow Hill and one to Paddington. There was one through freight in the evening, 7/00pm from Barmouth Junction due Ruabon at 11:56pm. There were the usual trips from Bala to Ruabon and Wrexham and beyond.

The British Railways edition for **September 1949** shows broadly the same pattern with the Down Mail departing Ruabon at 4.17am followed by the through freight at 4.45am. Five

BARMOUTH, DOLGELLEY, CORWEN, LLANGOLLEN AND RUABON.

Week Days. **Up Trains.**

STATIONS.	Ruling Gradient 1 in	Time Allowances for Ordinary Freight Tr'ns see page 2. Point-to-Point Times	Allow for Stop.	Allow for Start.	B Birkenhead Pass.	B Birkenhead Pass.	B Chest'r Auto.	K Frght	B Auto. SX	B Pass.	A B'ham Pass. X SO	A Padt'n Pass. J SO
		Mins.	Mins.	Mins.	a.m.	a.m.	a.m.	a.m.	a.m.	a.m.	a.m.	a.m.
BARMOUTH dep.								Arrive Bontnewydd 6.24.		7 18	8 10	8 45
Barmouth Junction arr.										7X23	—	8 50
Barmouth Junction dep.				1						7 24	8 15	8X53
Arthog ,,	L.	4	1	1						7 27	—	—
Penmaenpool ,,	132 R.P	13	1	1						7 39	CXS	CXS
DOLGELLEY arr.	200 R.	7	1							7 43	—	—
DOLGELLEY dep.	—	—	—	1		Depart Bala 7.17 a.m.		6 10	7 30	7 45	C8 40S	C9 12S
Dolserau Halt ,,	91 R.							—	7 36½	—	—	—
Bontnewydd ,,	91 R.	12	1	2				6 36	7 40	7 52	CS	CXS
Wnion Halt ,,	66 R.	—	—	—				—	7 46	7 58	—	—
Drws-y-Nant arr.	50 R.	17	1	2				6 56	7 52	8X 4	—	—
Drws-y-Nant dep.								7X 6		8 5	CS	CS
Garneddwen Halt, Loop & Stop Board arr.	58 R.	17	1	1				7X26	Will not run during school holidays.	W	—	—
Garneddwen Halt, Loop & Stop Board dep.								7P28		CS	CXS	CS
Llys Halt ,,	126 F.	—	—	—				—		8 15	—	—
Llanuwchllyn arr.	63 F.	8§	1	1				7 38		8 19	—	—
Llanuwchllyn dep.		(§ 9 minutes when exceeding Single Engine load.)						7P40		8 20	CS	CS
Flag Station ,,	71 F.							—		8 24	—	—
Llangower Halt ,,	264 F.							—		8 28	—	—
BALA JUNCTION arr.	220 R.	12	1	1		CS		70W54		8X33	SUSPENDED —	SUSPENDED —
BALA JUNCTION dep.						7 19		7 59		8 36	C9 15S	C9 55S
Llandderfel arr.	300 R.	8	1	1		7 25		—		8 42	—	—
Llandderfel dep.						7 26		C8 8		8 42½	CS	CS
Llandrillo arr.	200 R.	7	1	1		7 31		8 16		8 47½	—	—
Llandrillo dep.						7 32		8X30		8 48	CXS	CS
Cynwyd ,,	200 R.	7	1	1		7 38		CS		8 53	—	—
CORWEN arr.	L.	5	1	1		7 42		8 44		8 57	9O35	10OX15
CORWEN dep.						7 47		9 10		9 0	9W45	10W23
Bonwm Halt ,,	792 F.	—	—	—		7 50		—		E	—	—
Carrog ,,	300 R.	6	1	1		7X58		CS		9 6	—	—
Glyndyfrdwy arr.	352 F.	5	1	1		8 2		—		9 11	—	—
Glyndyfrdwy dep.						8 3		9CR22		9 12	CXS	CS
Deeside ,,	L.	5	1	1		—		—		—	—	—
Stop Board—Y ,,	180 R		1	1		—		—		—	—	—
Berwyn ,,	435 R.					8 12		—		9 21	—	—
LLANGOLLEN (Goods Junction) arr.	110 F.	7	2	1		CS		9 36		CS	—	—
LLANGOLLEN (Goods Junction) dep.					7†28	8 16		10 40		9 25	C10 4S	C10 41S
LLANGOLLEN (Pass'ger Station) arr.	80 F.	2	1	1	7†30	8 17		—		9 26	—	—
LLANGOLLEN (Pass'ger Station) dep.					7 35	8 19	9 10	—		9 28	10 5	10 42
Sun Bank Halt ,,	75 R.				—	—	—	—		—	—	—
Trevor ,,	75 R.	14	1	2	7 44	8 27	9 19	11 10		H	—	—
Acrefair ,,	85 R.	4	1	1	7 48	8 31	9 23	11 27		H	N	—
Stop Board ,,	54 F.	1	1	1	—	—	—	11P35		—	—	—
Llangollen Line Jct. ,,	75 F.	4			7 51	8 34	9 26	11P47		9 41	10 28	10 54
RUABON arr.	314 F.	3	1		7 53	8 36	9 28	11 51		9 43	10 30	10 56

STATIONS.	B Auto	A B'ham Pass. SO	K Frght	K 8.55 a.m. Bala Frght	B Pass. SO	B Pass.	K Frght SO	K Frght	A B'ham Pass. Z SO
	a.m.	a.m.	a.m.	a.m.	a.m.	a.m.	p.m.	a.m.	p.m.
BARMOUTH dep.	9 25	9 25				10 10			12 38
Barmouth Junction arr.	9 30	9 30				10 15			12 43
Barmouth Junction dep.	9 31	9 31				10 16		11 6	12 44
Arthog ,,	9 34	9 34				10 19		CR	12 47
Penmaenpool ,,	9X47	9X47				10 32		CR	1X 1
DOLGELLEY arr.	9 51	9 51				10 36		11X30	1 5
DOLGELLEY dep.		9 55			11.15 a.m. Bala to Wrexham. SUSPENDED	10 40		12 10	1 7
Dolserau Halt ,,		—				—		—	—
Bontnewydd ,,		CS				10 47		12 34	CS
Wnion Halt ,,		—				10 53		—	—
Drws-y-Nant arr.		—				10 59		12 54	—
Drws-y-Nant dep.		CS				11 0		1 4	CS
Garneddwen Halt, Loop & Stop Board arr.		—				11X 8		1P24	—
Garneddwen Halt, Loop & Stop Board dep.		CS				11W10		1 29	CS
Llys Halt ,,		—				11 14		—	—
Llanuwchllyn arr.		—				11 17½		1 39	—
Llanuwchllyn dep.		CS				11 18		1P49	CS
Flag Station ,,		—				11 22		—	—
Llangower Halt ,,		—				11 25		—	—
BALA JUNCTION arr.		SUSPENDED —				11 30		2 3	SUSPENDED —
BALA JUNCTION dep.		C10X40S	8	9* 4	11 17	11 33		2 11	C1 40S
Llandderfel arr.		—		9 13	11X23	11X39		Arrive Bala 2.15 p.m. For continuation see 4.1 p.m. Bala.	—
Llandderfel dep.		CS		9 23	11 23½	11 39½			CS
Llandrillo arr.		—		9 32	11X28½	11 44½			—
Llandrillo dep.		CS		9X40	11 29	11 45			CXS
Cynwyd ,,		—	Arr. Stop Board 11.58 a.m., Llangollen Line Junction 12.8 p.m.	CR	11 34	11 50	Arrive Acrefair 2.25 p.m.		—
CORWEN arr.		—		9 54	11X38	11 54			—
CORWEN dep.		C11 0S		12X20	11 40	11 56			CXS
Bonwm Halt ,,		—		—	—	—			—
Carrog ,,		—		12 45	11 46	12 1½			—
Glyndyfrdwy arr.		—		12 52	11 50	12 6			—
Glyndyfrdwy dep.		CS		1 2	11 51	12 6½			CS
Deeside ,,		—		CS	—	—			CXS
Stop Board—Y ,,		—		—	—	—			—
Berwyn ,,		—		—	12 0	12 15			—
LLANGOLLEN (Goods Junction) arr.		CS		1X17	—	CS			—
LLANGOLLEN (Goods Junction) dep.		11X17		2 30	C12 4S	12 19			C2 42S
LLANGOLLEN (Pass'ger Station) arr.		—		—	12 5	12 20			—
LLANGOLLEN (Pass'ger Station) dep.		11 18		—	12 8	12 21			2 43
Sun Bank Halt ,,		—		—	—	—			—
Trevor ,,		—	11 50	CR	12 16	12 29	2 15		—
Acrefair ,,		—	CR M	—	12 20	12 33	2 45		—
Stop Board ,,		—	12P 3	2P58	—	—	2P50		—
Llangollen Line Jct. ,,		11 33	12P13	3P 6	12 23	12 36	2P55		2 58
RUABON arr.		11 35	12 18	3 10	12 25	12 38	2 59		3 0

E—Calls if required to pick up on notice to the Station Master at Corwen. H—Calls to set down only on notice to Guard at Llangollen. J—7.15 a.m. ex Pwllheli. M—CR Acrefair, or Bowers Siding. N—10 minutes recovery time allowed, Llangollen to Ruabon. W—See note, page 141. X—7.15 a.m. ex Criccieth. Z—11.5 a.m. ex Pwllheli.

BARMOUTH, DOLGELLEY, CORWEN, LLANGOLLEN & RUABON Up Trains—continued.

WEEK DAYS.

STATIONS.	B Pass. SO	B Pass.	A Wrexham Pass.	B 3.25 p.m. Auto Bala to Wrexham.	B Birkenhead Pass.	D Empty Auto SX ¶ RR	D Empty C'ches. to Bala. SX	B Pass. SX R	K Frght C
	p.m.	p.m.	p.m.	p.m.	p.m.	p.m.	p.m.	p.m.	p.m.
BARMOUTH dep.	12 38	12 50	1 12		2 36	3 0			
Barmouth Junction arr.	12 43	12 55	1 17		2 41	3 7			
Barmouth Junction dep.	12 44	12 58	1 18		2 42	3 15			
Arthog ,,	12 47	1 1	—		2 45	—	R		
Penmaenpool ,,	1X 1	1 14	1Z 31		2 58	CS			
DOLGELLEY arr.	1 5	1 18	1 36		3 2	3 33			
DOLGELLEY dep.	SUSPENDED Third Class only.	Third Class only.	1 38		3 5			4X25	Continuation of 11.6 a.m. ex Barmouth Jct. Alternative times when not required to call between Bala and Corwen.
Dolserau Halt ,,			—		—			4 31	
Bontnewydd ,,			1 45		3 12			4 39	
Wnion Halt ,,			—		3 18			4 45	
Drws-y-Nant arr.			1 55		3 24			4 51	
Drws-y-Nant dep.			1 56		3 25				
Garneddwen Halt, Loop & Stop Board arr.			—		CS				
Garneddwen Halt, Loop & Stop Board dep.			—		W		4†20		
Llys Halt ,,			—		3 35	K Frght SX p.m.	—		
Llanuwchllyn arr.			2 8		3 38½		—		
Llanuwchllyn dep.			2 9		3X39		CS		
Flag Station ,,			—		3 43		—		
Llangower Halt ,,			—		3 46		—		
BALA JUNCTION arr.			2 18		3X51		4†36		
BALA JUNCTION dep.			2 21	3 27	3 54		4†40		4 11
Llandderfel arr.			2 Z27	3 33	4 0		See Note A.		—
Llandderfel dep.			CXS	3 34	4 1				C4 19S
Llandrillo arr.			—	3 39	4X 6				4 27
Llandrillo dep.			2 Z31	3 40	4 7				4X31
Cynwyd ,,			—	3 46	U	Arr. Acrefair 5.18 p.m., Stop Board 5.31 p.m., Llangollen Line Jct. 5.42 p.m.			4 39
CORWEN arr.			2 40	3 50	4 17				4X45
CORWEN dep.			2 42	3 54	4X21				5 47
Bonwm Halt ,,			—	3 57	U			B Ruabon Pass.	—
Carrog ,,			CXS	4 2	4 30				—
Glyndyfrdwy arr.			—	4 6	4 35				C5 59S
Glyndyfrdwy dep.			—	4X 7	4X36				—
Deeside ,,			—	—	—				—
Stop Board—Y ,,			—	—	—				—
Berwyn ,,			—	4 16	U				—
LLANGOLLEN (Goods Junction) arr.			CS	CS	CS			p.m.	6*13
LLANGOLLEN (Goods Junction) dep.			3 1	4X20	4 49			5†32	6 53
LLANGOLLEN (Passenger Station) arr.			3 2	4 21	4 50			5†34	—
LLANGOLLEN (Passenger Station) dep.			3‡ 7	4 24	4 55			5 40	—
Sun Bank Halt ,,			—	—	—				—
Trevor ,,			—	4 33	5 5	5 11		5 48	—
Acrefair ,,			—	4 37	5 10	5 28		5 52	—
Stop Board ,,			—	—	H	5P36		—	7P20
Llangollen Line Jct. ,,			3 18	4 40	5 18	5P47		5 55	7P31
RUABON arr.			3 20	4 42	5 20	5 52		5 57	7 36

STATIONS.	K Frght C	B Wrexham Pass.	B Auto.	K Frght SX	B Pass. Mail.	K Frght X	B Auto. SX	B Auto. SO	G Light Engine
	p.m.	p.m.	p.m.	p.m.	p.m.	p.m.	p.m.	p.m.	p.m.
BARMOUTH dep.			5 46		7 20		8 51	9 40	10 0
Barmouth Junction arr.			5 51		7 25		8 56	9 45	—
Barmouth Junction dep.			5 52		7 26	7 0	8 57	9 46	10 6
Arthog ,,			5 55		7 29	—	9 0	9 49	—
Penmaenpool ,,			6 8		7 42	—	9X13	10 2	10 20
DOLGELLEY arr.			6 12		7 46	7 25	9 17	10 6	
DOLGELLEY dep.	Continuation of 11.6 a.m. ex Barmouth Jct.	Bala depart 5.45 p.m.			7 49	8 10			After working 6.55 p.m. Ruabon to Barmouth.
Dolserau Halt ,,					7B054	—			
Bontnewydd ,,					7 58	CS			
Wnion Halt ,,					8 4	—			
Drws-y-Nant arr.					8 10	8 41			
Drws-y-Nant dep.					8 11	8X48			
Garneddwen Halt, Loop & Stop Board arr.					—	CS			
Garneddwen Halt, Loop & Stop Board dep.					8 17	9P13			
Llys Halt ,,					8 21	—			
Llanuwchllyn arr.					8 25	P			
Llanuwchllyn dep.					8X26	CS			
Flag Station ,,					8 30	—			
Llangower Halt ,,					8 33	—			
BALA JUNCTION arr.					8 38	9 35			
BALA JUNCTION dep.	4 4	5 47			8 43	10 0			
Llandderfel arr.	4 13	5 53	B Auto.		8 49	10 9			
Llandderfel dep.	4 18	5 54			8 50	10 15			
Llandrillo arr.	4X27	5 59			8 55	B10 24			
Llandrillo dep.	4 33	6 0			8 56	B10X27			
Cynwyd ,,	4 47D	6 5		Arrive Acrefair 7.39 p.m. Arrive Stop Board 7.52 p.m. Arr. Llangollen Line Jct. 8.3 p.m.	9 1	—			
CORWEN arr.	4X54	6 9	p.m.		9 5	10 41			
CORWEN dep.	5 47	6 10	6 45		9 7	10 50			
Bonwm Halt ,,	—	6 13	—		—	—			
Carrog ,,	—	6 17	6 51		9 13	—			
Glyndyfrdwy arr.	C5 59S	6 21	6 55		9 17½	—			
Glyndyfrdwy dep.	—	6 22	6 56		9 19	CS			
Deeside ,,	—	—	SUSPENDED		—	—			
Stop Board—Y ,,	—	—			—	—			
Berwyn ,,	—	6 31			—	—			
LLANGOLLEN (Goods Junction) arr.	6*13	CS	CS		—	—			
LLANGOLLEN (Goods Junction) dep.	6 53	6 35	7 8		9 31	C11 14S			
LLANGOLLEN (Passenger Station) arr.	—	6 36	7 9		9 32	—			
LLANGOLLEN (Passenger Station) dep.	—	6 37	7 10		9 35	—			
Sun Bank Halt ,,	—	—	—		—	—			
Trevor ,,	—	6 45	7 19	7 32	9 44	E			
Acrefair ,,	—	6 49	7 24	7 49	9 49	—			
Stop Board ,,	7P20	—	—	7P57	—	11P38			
Llangollen Line Jct. ,,	7P31	6 52	7 27	8P*8	9 52	11P45			
RUABON arr.	7 36	6 54	7 29	8 13	9 54	11 50			

A—Must not be allowed to delay 3.45 p.m. Ruabon to Barmouth. Crossing of these trains to be regulated accordingly.
B—On Saturdays Llandrillo C10 33S, Corwen 10.36X10.50 p.m.
C—Arrive Stop Board, 6.33 p.m., Llangollen Line Junction 6.44 p.m.
D—Arrive Cynwyd 4.42 p.m.
E—Arrive Stop Board 11.36 p.m., Llangollen Line Junction 11.43 p.m.
H—Five minutes recovery time allowed.
R—Will not run during School Holidays.
U—Calls to set down passengers from Bala and Llanuwchllyn and beyond on notice to Guard at Bala Junction.
W—See note on page 141.
X—Bala 9.41/9.57 p.m.
Y—Trains of more than 20 wagons Mineral, 25 Mineral and Freight, 30 Freight, or 40 Empties, must stop dead at Glyndyfrdwy end of Berwyn Tunnel and pin down brakes before descending the incline to tunnel.
Z—Calls only if required to pick up passengers for beyond Ruabon.
‡—Advertised Llangollen depart 3.2 p.m.
¶—Saturdays and School Holidays excepted.

LIST OF SIGNAL BOXES

RUABON AND DOLGELLEY.

—	—	Acrefair		6. 0 a.m.	6. 0 a.m.	K 6.45 a.m.	—	—	Yes.
1	7¾	Trevor		4.30 a.m.	4.30 a.m.	7.10 p.m.§	—	—	Yes.
3	44	Llangollen Station		—	—	—	—	—	
—	44	Llangollen Goods Junction	A	4. 0 a.m.	4. 0 a.m.	11.30 p.m.	—	—	No.
2	63¼	Deeside		2.15 p.m.	2.15 p.m.	5. 0 p.m.	—	—	Yes.
1	72¾	Glyndyfrdwy	A	4.15 a.m.	4.15 a.m.	11. 0 p.m.	—	—	No.
2	9¾	Carrog N		7.40 a.m. 2.20 p.m.	7.40 a.m. 2.20 p.m.	9. 0 a.m. 5. 0 p.m.	—	—	Yes.
2	65¼	Corwen, East	A	4.30 a.m.	4.30 a.m.	11. 5 p.m.	—	—	No.
—	27¼	Corwen, West	A	4.50 a.m.	4.50 a.m.	11. 0 p.m.	—	—	No.
4	31¾	Llandrillo	A	4.50 a.m.	4.50 a.m.	11. 0 p.m.	—	—	No.
2	60½	Llandderfel	A	5. 0 a.m.	5. 0 a.m.	10.45 p.m.	—	—	No.
3	33⅛	Bala Junction	A	5. 5 a.m.	5. 5 a.m.	10.50 p.m.	—	—	No.
4	79	Llanuwchllyn	A	5.15 a.m.	5.15 a.m.	10. 0 p.m.	—	—	No.
2	70	Garneddwen Loop		9.20 a.m. —	9.20 a.m. 8.30 a.m.	4.40 p.m.SX 4.40 p.m.SO	—	—	Yes.
3	31½	Drws-y-Nant	A	5.30 a.m.	5.30 a.m.	9.40 p.m.	—	—	No.
3	53	Bontnewydd	A	5.40 a.m.	5.40 a.m.	9.10 p.m.	—	—	No.
3	2	Dolgelley Station	A	5.25 a.m. —	5.25 a.m. —	9.40 p.m.SX 10.30 p.m.SO	—	—	No.
2	15	Penmaenpool	A	5.15 a.m.	5.15 a.m.	10.45 p.m.	—	—	No.

A—To close after last Train has cleared.
K—Also as required during day.
N—Or when advised by Corwen East or Glyndyfrdwy.
§—or when 7.32 p.m. Freight has left.

BALA JUNCTION AND BLAENAU FESTINIOG.

0	0	Bala Junction		—	See	above.	—	—	No.
0	54	Bala	A	5. 0 a.m.	5. 0 a.m.	11. 0 p.m.	—	—	No.
2	48	Frongoch	A	6.35 a.m.	6.35 a.m.	8*40 p.m.	(*9.25 p.	m. Sats.)	No.
5	11¼	Arenig		6.35 a.m.	6.35 a.m.	8*30 p.m.	(*9.50 p.	m. Sats.)	No.
2	59½	Cwm Prysor		As require	d.				Yes.
5	73¼	Trawsfynydd	A	*6. 0 a.m.	6. 0 a.m.	8*15 p.m.	(*11.10 p	m. Sats.)	No.
4	78	Festiniog	A	*6. 0 a.m.	6. 0 a.m.	8*0 p.m.	(*10.55 p.	m. Sats.)	No.
3	23	Blaenau Festiniog	A	*6.15 a.m.	6.15 a.m.	7*35 p.m.	(*10.40 p.	m. Sats.)	No.

*—Opens correspondingly later when Workmen's Train retimed.
A—To close after last train has cleared.

through trains ran daily SX. again some running through to Pwllheli. The 7.50am through freight also ran to Barmouth Junction and arrived there at 4/21pm. Some **Saturdays Only** trains are shown but those were listed as conditional. Nevertheless, they ran when Butlins Holiday Camp at Penychain was open. There were the regular short distance freight and auto trains operating in approximately the same timings. The early morning freight from Dolgellau departed at 6.10am and the first passenger left Barmouth at 7.18am due Ruabon at 9.43am. The passenger overtook the freight at Corwen where the Penmaenpool freight train crew handed over and travelled back home "on the cushions". There were five passenger trains every weekday between Barmouth and Ruabon or beyond including the ever faithful evening Mail departing this time at 7/20pm. The evening through freight from Barmouth Junction left there at 7/00pm and arrived Ruabon at 11/50pm.

The BR Standard Working Time Table design was introduced to the Chester and Oswestry Divisions on 19th.September 1955. Passenger and freight traffic was listed in separate books. Chester District was designated Western Region section J. Oswestry district, which covered the Cambrian Coast became section L but continued to show passenger and freight traffic in the same book, which made life easier for all concerned. The first section J issues to hand are dated 11th June 1956 for both passenger and freight traffic. The Mail train continued to run but as it was a Class "F" working, was not listed in the passenger book but is shown with the freight workings. There were six through passenger workings SX. with eight on a Saturday. Also shown in the time tables were the LM Region Land Cruise trains which ran Tuesdays to Fridays in the season. The Time Table was as unimaginative as ever and many of the short journey workings had disappeared. There was still some auto coach workings between Ruabon and Llangollen or Bala, but these were reduced to a minimum. In the Up direction the same five trains ran with marginally adjusted timings. Life didn't change much on the line over the years. On Saturdays the number of trains was increased to seven.

The following summer the page layout of the WTT was rotated through ninety degrees, which meant that the whole spread could be read more easily. The number of trains had dropped back to five through workings daily SX, with eight through trains SO. In the Up direction the pattern remained unchanged from the previous year with the same short journeys running in the same timings. By the summer of 1959 the number of through trains had dropped to four in both directions. By June 1962 this had increased to five Down trains, but still only four Up trains.

The Down freight services shown for 1960 were three through trains including the Mail to Barmouth or Barmouth Junction, now called Morfa Mawddach. The last one of the three ran SX. On Saturdays Only a freight departed from Croes Newydd yard which by now had taken over most of Ruabon yard functions, and this turn ran to Dolgellau. In the Up direction there were two through trains, one in mid morning which ran daily with different intermediate timings on Saturdays, but still arriving back at Croes Newydd yard at the same finishing time, and the evening freight, 6/42pm ex Morfa Mawddach, passing Ruabon Middle signalbox at 11/06pm. By June 1961 the evening freight to Croes Newydd yard had become SX. and the same timings persisted into the summer of 1962.

In 1963 the former Great Western Railway Shrewsbury, Chester and Oswestry District lines in North and Mid Wales were transferred en block to the London Midland Region Western Division. The Down line trains had again increased to five through workings with four in the Up direction. The final summer workings for **1964** showed no change of pattern in the passenger workings with five through trains Down line and four Up line. The freight work was trimmed back to the Mails, working 3.20am MX. and 3.30am MO from Croes Newydd yard to Barmouth, with only one working SX at 6.05am from Croes Newydd to Bala and two workings, one SX to Trevor. In the Up direction there were no through workings, only one SX, working from Bala at 09.33am and two return workings, one SX. from Trevor to Croes Newydd.

The final timetable for the line dated **7th.September 1964 to 13th.June 1965** shows four through workings from Wrexham or Chester to Barmouth or Pwllheli, with no variations on a Saturday but with one afternoon working from Wrexham to Bala. At last the numbers of Up direction trains balanced the Down workings, four in each direction. One train worked through from Pwllheli to Chester and Birkenhead, and the one return working from Bala to Wrexham General. Services were withdrawn from Monday 2nd November 1964, only to be reinstated on 23rd November due to a failure to provide alternative bus services. However on 12th December 1964 flooding washed away part of the track near Llandderfel and services were then withdrawn again. Emergency bus services were provided between Llangollen and Bala. Trains resumed running between Wrexham, Ruabon and Llangollen until 18th January 1965 when they finally ceased. The same situation affected the western end of the line. Rail services were restored between Bala, Bala Junction, Dolgellau and Barmouth but ultimately withdrawn on the same date. The track remained in situ until 1967 when demolition commenced on either side of the broached track at Llandderfel. Demolition trains working east stopped at Llangollen Goods Line Junction where a buffer stop was installed. There was still a reasonable quantity of freight being handled at Llangollen, mainly from the Carters Seed Factory, and so the Llangollen

freight trip lingered, but eventually this too succumbed and the line closed on 1st.April 1968, the last four months traffic being limited to coal deliveries. The track was subsequently removed. The line remained double track between Llangollen Line Junction and Llangollen Goods Junction during this period, and although it was proposed the short section between Acrefair and Llangollen Line Junction be singled this was never done.

MOTIVE POWER

The line remained steam worked for regular traffic throughout its entire life although latterly, Diesel Multiple Units made regular visits along the Denbigh Ruthin & Corwen line on excursion trains from Llandudno and occasional workings from the Midlands and the Potteries during the summer months.

For most of its life, GWR locomotives worked the line, and the route limit was yellow classification which precluded all but the lightest of weight tender and tank locomotives. In the period between the wars certain structures were renovated and so this enabled the route to be upgraded to blue category enabling that classification of locomotives to work through to Barmouth. Originally, the shorter trips were worked by tank locomotives of the saddletank or pannier variety, whilst 2-4-0, 4-4-0 and 0-6-0 tender engines performed on the through working to Barmouth. After the first upgrading of the line in 1927, 43xx class 2-6-0 tender locomotives were authorised to work through, and ultimately, so were the 78xx Manor class locomotives. Although some class 31xx class 2-6-2Ts were authorised, and there are recorded instances when they worked part of the route, their limited water capacity generally precluded them from working over the whole route. For the same reason, the 45xx class 2-6-2Ts also ruled themselves out on water capacity but in the event, the bunker payload would have given little margin of safety. After nationalization, British Railways standard classes 2, 3 and 4 tender and tank locomotives were authorised, and did take over some of the duties. These were usually the 80xxx class 4 tanks and

9. Bonwm. An Up Class A train nears Bonwm Halt, headed by No.**7823** *Hook Norton Manor*. Mr.C.B.Collett designed the class especially for this type of secondary main line duty, introducing them from 1938 onwards. Calculated at 85% of the working boiler pressure of 225 lb.sq.in. the Tractive Effort of the Manor Class was 27,430 lbs., putting them in Power Class D. Consequently a Route Restriction Colour, Blue, indicated by the Letter D was displayed on a coloured disc affixed to the cab-side.
Photo: John Keylock.

75xxx tender engines on through workings, with ex LMS 2-6-4T making appearances from time to time. Certainly when the lines were transferred to the L.M. Region, these classes appeared more frequently with Ivatt class 2-6-0 tender and 2-6-2T tank versions being seen regularly. 41204 was based at Bala to work the shuttle between the Junction and Town stations for some time, whilst 46521 was resident at Penmaenpool to work the Dolgellau to Barmouth trips. Nevertheless, such workings were confined to the period after 1960, and up to that time the only appearance of LMS engines was with the Land Cruise workings in the 1950s. LMS 4-6-0 class 5 tender engines were alleged to have been seen at Corwen but such reports are unconfirmed.

Initially, on the Denbigh to Corwen line, LNWR locomotives reigned supreme but in time gave up their exclusive preserve. From LMS to early BR days when the Denbigh to Corwen line was open for passenger traffic, Standard class 2P 4-4-0 tender engines worked the line regularly on the passenger services and examples were based at Denbigh and Rhyl. Occasionally, a Chester based class 4P 4-4-0 Compound made an appearance. The LNWR, and later the LMS, had an outstation at Corwen and Denbigh based 2-4-2T's of Webb design were the usual performers. After the 1927 General Strike the workings changed when the LMS closed their out-station at Corwen. The freight turns were worked by LNWR 0-6-0 tender coal engines which were superceded by Midland design 0-6-0 Class 3F. Latterly, the B.R. Class 2 2-6-0 tender engines of 78xxx class took over the duty. Freight traffic was interchanged daily, Saturdays included, with the Western at Corwen. There were two Freight trips daily prior to 1933 but this was cut back to one some time after that date. Starting from Denbigh about 9.30am [times varied over the years] it was a leisurely and protracted working taking some ten hours for the round trip which even in those days was considered to be excessive for the train crews. Until the passenger traffic ceased, Denbigh shed crews changed footplates at Corwen so that the crew who worked the Down morning freight returned with a passenger trip and vice versa. The GWR motive power facilities were located originally at Corwen, Bala and Dolgellau with working from the eastern end of the line originating from Wrexham (Croes Newydd) shed. As already stated, the Motive Power Department at Corwen closed in 1927 and it may well have been the GWR closure which caused the LMS to follow suit. Nevertheless, the turntable and water columns were retained in the Up side freight yard at the western (Dolgellau) end of the station. It is believed [but not confirmed] that the Motive Power staff from Corwen were transferred either to Croes Newydd or to Bala. Certainly the traffic returns suggest that Bala traffic staff increased between 1923 and 1931 which was against the current trend for this time.

The largest depot in the district was Wrexham Croes Newydd and the make-up of the shed provided three links after the war. Number One link comprised 12 sets of men who by their seniority had the pick of the workings. Such was the nature of the drivers there that they preferred to contain their wanderings to Birkenhead via Chester, to Barmouth and Shrewsbury. Their earliest turn started about 5.00am, and their latest finish was not much after 10.30pm according to information supplied by former drivers R.Cartwright and T.Roberts. Number Two link at Croes Newydd worked further afield and comprised twenty six sets of men working to Wolverhampton, Barmouth, Chester and Birkenhead as well as the branch lines around Wrexham. Number three link comprised twelve sets of men who worked the local trip workings, pilot duties and shunting turns on the various yards in the Wrexham area, as well as preparation and disposal duties. There was an 'Old Mans' link which catered for drivers who were recovering from illness or who, due to various circumstances were restricted to light duties. Their work included the various turning duties and those confined to shed limits. The auto train workings were mostly located in No.2 link although there were one or two trips on the units in No.3 link. Most of No.2 link work was freight and about half the duties were night time workings. The diagrammed work for the District was dominated by Chester and Shrewsbury sheds, both of which were much larger than Croes Newydd, and subsequently much of the work started or terminated there.

Before the war, Croes Newydd men had two lodging turns to Oxley Sidings, working both ways with freight workings. Men also signed for the road as far as Oxford but this was discontinued at the commencement of WW2 and never reinstated. It has been suggested that the senior men did not want to return to the pre-war duties which they considered arduous, but preferred to leave the mileage turns for distant locations to Chester shed, who regularly worked to Oxford after the war. Before 1939, Chester shed had regular turns working to Paddington.

The smaller sub sheds to Croes Newydd had no link structure and the men worked around the duties in rotation. All

10. Penmaenpool. c.**1963**. The driver of 4MT No.**75006**, a Croes Newydd (89B) engine, on a Down Class B train, confers with the signalman at Penmaenpool in a scene which suggests light activity, at the sight of open carriage doors and a 'busy' platform. 'Half-harp' shaped lighting columns are observed on Up and Down platforms. The Down shelter, its single-pitch roof extended to form a rudimentary awning, actually stands in the goods yard, where we note coal wagons in the siding. Coal traffic was the mainstay of the yard which was closed from the 4th May 1964.
Photo: C.L.Caddy.

sheds on the line were outstations to Croes Newydd who undertook all repair work, and locomotives worked to the home shed for washout and maintenance as a normal part of their diagrams.

Trawsfynydd duties were usually worked by pannier tank 0-6-0 locomotives, and two were normally out-sta-tioned there. There was no separate shed but according to E.Lyons in his standard work on GWR Sheds, there was a brick walled slate roofed lean-to adjoining the goods shed. In 1947 it housed pannier tank no.1706, but the allocation was arbitrary. It is understood that four sets of men were based here about this time although by the closure date this had been cut back to two sets.

Bala shed at the other end of the branch was con-structed of brick with a slate roof and with a water tank surmounting the shed entrance. In 1947 there were four 0-6-0PT's shedded there, numbers 1773, 7403, 7409 and 7414 together with 0-4-2T's 5810 and 5811. The panniers were involved in cyclic working between Croes Newydd and Trawsfynydd, and could appear on any of the three depots working diagrams. The 0-4-2Ts were used on auto-train workings between Bala and Wrexham. Nevertheless the crews were not confined to tank engine working and part of one diagram included an afternoon working to Croes Newydd with a 43xx class 2-6-0 class. One of the Croes Newydd fleet arrived daily and was serviced on Bala shed, the Bala men working out with the early afternoon freight to Ruabon yard.

Bala men signed for the road to Blaenau Ffestiniog, Pwllheli and Chester, whilst Trawsfynydd men, who worked most of the services on the Ffestiniog line, signed for their own branch, to Ruabon and to Wrexham.

Penmaenpool shed was constructed by the Cam-brian Railways to work their service from Dolgellau to Barmouth but with the amalgamation it became an anach-ronism. Its work still provided crews for the Dolgellau to Barmouth shuttle, generally worked by auto trains, and the men gained some freight workings to Corwen. The crews based here signed for the road as far as Wrexham and Pwllheli and worked regularly to Ruabon with summer sea-sonal relief trains. In its heyday, Penmaenpool had nine rostered turns but latterly this was reduced to four sets. At one time following a reappraisal of the workings, it was proposed [but not confirmed] that crews from the shed learned and signed for the coast road as far south as Towyn , and for the lines to Wrexham and Croes Newydd yards. They worked routinely to Bala and into Trevor yard as far as the Canal Basin. Nevertheless, until the end, the bulk of the work passing through Dolgellau was under-taken by crews from the eastern end of the line.

Penmaenpool also had 0-4-2Ts to work the auto train shuttle between Dolgellau and Barmouth and two sets of men worked throughout the day on what could have been a some-what monotonous duty. This was livened up morning and after-noon by an ECS working to Drws y Coed in the morning to bring children down to school at Dolgellau. The second set subse-quently returned the pupils in the afternoon. At one time in the late 1950s, one set would work a Saturdays only service from Barmouth to Ruabon with a through train to Birmingham, the stock reversing at Ruabon where the Penmaenpool men were relieved. The locomotive would normally be a 43xx class 2-6-0 but

11. Bontnewydd. c.1963. A tourist's view of the Wnion Valley with balmy skies and rural stations as No.**75006** calls with a Down stopping train. However, on Saturday and Sunday, the 12th and 13th December 1964, the Afon Wnion burst its banks, flooding Dolgellau Station and its surroundings, interrupting services for several hours. *Photo: C.L.Caddy.*

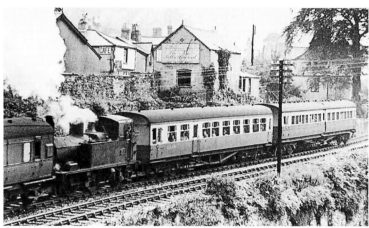

12. Llangollen. 10th June 1952. (Tuesday). An 0-4-2T leaves Llangollen with a Bala to Wrexham auto-train. At the turn of the century the G.W.R. en-thusiastically adopted the rail-car idea, and eventually had the largest fleet of any. History though relates that the inflexibility of the units worked against the idea and the versatile "push-pull" replaced them to become the 'motor-train' of the branch lines. *Photo: W.G.Rear.*

occasionally a Manor would be rostered. If the loadings were particularly heavy the job would be double headed and various permutations would present themselves.

For many years there were seven sets of men at Penmaen-pool, and according to J.P.Richards who lived nearby, the stan-dard of engine working was high. As the work contracted the younger members transferred away or left the service and by 1963 only four sets were left.

The Engine and Enginemens Working sheets issued in September 1963 and supplied by Roland Pittard of Bridgend, the work was as follows:

Turn No.**1**. was a Locomotive turn, worked daily, Mon-day to Saturdays and was marked for a 465XX covering four round trips on the Dolgellau to Barmouth shuttle. Traincrew turn No.**5**. would work one trip to Barmouth and back and then spend from 10.15am until 12/00pm shunting at Dolgellau. They then worked the 1/41pm to Barmouth as far as Penmaenpool, where the traincrew were relieved by turn No.**8**. which worked three trips on the shuttle before parking the stock at Dolgellau and returning L.E. to the shed. There was a variation of finishing

13. **Penmaenpool. c.1963.** The most noticeable feature of the move from a G.W.R. aligned operation to an L.M.R. orientated control was the disappearance of the familiar 'Western' engines, and to a Penmaenpool, little changed since its re-construction in the 1920's, comes No.**75006** with a Class A working for Ruabon and Birkenhead, conveying "through" coaches for Euston. The Down side Picking Up post can be seen opposite the signal box. The relevant equipment for the Up side was 120 yards on the Dolgellau side of the box. However, the signalman is on the platform waiting to effect the token exchange manually. Note the open-fronted trestle platform, the river bank supporting the structural members and the heaped ballast, formed to prevent erosion at high-water. On the extreme left, the Down siding comes in to join the Down main line at Point 15, F.P.L. No.13. Penmaenpool level crossing was exempt from the provisions of Rule 99A "Gates across public road," special instructions applying to its operation.
Photo: C.L.Caddy.

time on a Saturday. Traincrew turn No.**7**. came on duty at 5.15am and prepared the overnight engine, Croes Newydd locomotive turn No.**4**. They worked light engine to Barmouth [0B08] where they changed footplates at 6.30am with Croes Newydd men working turn **26**, which was the 3.20am ex Chester. The men worked as required with the engine until 10.10am when they changed footplates again, this time with Croes Newydd men working turn No.**27** [Croes Newydd Locomotive turn No.**2**.], and shunted at Barmouth until 12/15pm. They were relieved at that time by Machynlleth men working turn No.**30**. and travelled back to Penmaenpool by the 1/00pm bus and signed off duty at 1/57pm.

Traincrew turn No.**6**. signed on duty at 2/45pm and prepared their engine, which was Croes Newydd Loco turn No.**3**. and went L.E. to Barmouth where they assembled the freight 6J02 and departed Barmouth at 5/15pm [Monday-Friday] to Bala Junction where they changed footplates with Croes

Newydd men working turn No.**25** [5/07pm Birkenhead to Barmouth passenger] with Croes Newydd loco turn No.**4**. which they took to Barmouth where they parked the coaches and went L.E. back to Penmaenpool. On Saturdays they departed Barmouth at 5/32pm for Dolgellau with the 9B29 and the same locomotive. They then attached to the front of the 7/15pm to Chester and worked as far as Llanuwchllyn before changing footplates with the same Croes Newydd men, turn No.**25**. on the same working, and took the passenger to Barmouth, parked stock and back L.E. to Penmaenpool.

Both Pwllheli and Portmadoc traincrews signed for the road as far as Corwen and regularly worked over the line in the summer season.

The D.M.U. workings over the line from Llandudno were confined to Tuesdays and Thursdays Only in the Summer season, running as excursion trips between 1958 and 1961, and operated initially with a pair of 2 coach Derby C.& W. lightweight

14.Llanuwchllyn. 19th May 1962. (Saturday). A definitive view of Llanuwchllyn, with the dapper figure of Station Master Mr.D.S.Evans, supervising operations. To his right are the smoke-blackened water tank and braziers, signs of a hard winter. On Mondays to Fridays, loco-men exchanged turns at Bala Junction, but on Saturdays this procedure took place at Llanuwchllyn. The Penmaenpool men who had worked No.**75006** forward with a Class B train for Chester, have crossed to the Down platform, where they will relieve Croes Newydd men who have worked the Down train to Barmouth. On the extreme left, note the Down 'Picking Up' post 32 yards on the Bala Junction side of the signal box. Winter could seriously disrupt the services and in 1947 Bala Lake was frozen to a great depth, the Station Master at Llanuwchllyn, during blizzard conditions, was under instructions to keep the Bala Station Master and the District Traffic Inspector at Corwen fully advised by telegram. Furthermore, in certain circumstances, the Station Masters at Dolgellau, Drws-y-Nant, Llanuwchllyn and Bala were authorised not to allow trains into forward sections.
Photo: C.L.Caddy.

units although these were replaced in the final season by what became class 108 units. The venture rejoiced under the title "The Clwyd Ranger" and which departed Llandudno at 2/30pm to Rhyl, where it reversed and traversed the Vale of Clwyd line to St.Asaph and Denbigh. It continued along through Ruthin to Corwen, where it arrived at 4/20pm. The return journey left Corwen at 4/55pm and followed the same route to Rhyl, where it reversed once more before proceeding along the coast, arriving back in Llandudno at 7/25pm. The working was covered by Rhyl men throughout.

D.M.U. excursions were run most days including Sundays but not Saturdays from the Potteries over the line to Barmouth between 1960 and 1963 during Stoke Wakes Holidays [the first two weeks in August], departing Uttoxeter at 8.42am and picking up at Blythe Bridge, Meir, Normacot, Longton, Stoke-on-Trent, Etruria, Longport, Kidsgrove Central and Alsager before proceeding to Chester, where a Chester No.1. link driver and guard relieved the Stoke crew and ran non-stop to Llangollen, [11.20am] Bala Lake Halt, [12/09pm], Dolgellau, [12/42pm] arriving at Barmouth at 1/10pm. The return working left Barmouth at 6/38pm and stopped at the same points before running non-stop to Chester, where Crewe men took over the working. According to John Roberts, former signalman at Llanuwchllyn, Trans-Pennine units worked the duty one season, and three two coach Birmingham C.& W. units made up the stock at other times. From time to time other D.M.U. workings ran over part or the whole of the line but not on a regular basis.

Diesel locomotives were rarely seen beyond Llangollen, until demolition commenced. Nevertheless Mr.Roberts photographed Class 24 Bo-Bo on a freight working by Llyn Tegid, and there is an unconfirmed report from Frank Parish, signalman on the Bala Lake Railway, of a similar locomotive working the daily through freight on at least one occasion in 1963 when there was a shortage of steam locomotives at Croes Newydd. During demolition, the same class of locomotives performed their melancholy duty working from Morfa Mawddach to and from the rail-head with Machynlleth or Pwllheli men at the controls.

COACH WORKING

The through coach working arrangements for passenger stock which travelled between Ruabon and Barmouth were somewhat unusual in that these regular passenger stock workings were undertaken with Central Wales District coaches and were shown in that Districts' programme. The workings from Birmingham and Paddington, which were normally confined to the summer period were undertaken with Class A workings, which were to be found in the 'Programme of Working of Coaches and Vans in Through Trains'. The Central Wales Programme also included the Auto Coach working between Barmouth and Dolgellau, and which was a hark back to the Cambrian days. The other Auto Coach Workings which started/finished at Bala, Llangollen, Ruabon,Wrexham or Chester, were shown in the Chester District Programme. Only one set of coaches from the Chester District was involved otherwise and

15. Corwen. c.1963. Strong shadows enhance this view of the east end of Corwen station, with a B.R. 4MT 4-6-0 in charge of an Up train. To the right of the engine is the well known scissors crossover, utilized by trains off the Denbigh line. Between East and West signal boxes, the controlling movements were from Up Main to Down Main,F.P.L. No.15, Points No.13A and 13B, F.P.L. No.14. Down Main to Up Main. Points No.12 and No.11. F.P.L. No.14. The 'road' is actually set for the former LNW/LMS line. *Photo: C.L.Caddy.*

16. Corwen. A Derby built Multiple-Unit, then in the forefront of modernisation, was photographed working a Society Special at Corwen. The footbridge, which had its dilapidated roof covering removed in the 1950's, provided a fine vantage point for the photographers, whilst other enthusiasts explore the now sadly, abandoned platform. *Photo: C.L.Caddy.*

that was the early morning Bala to Birkenhead working which also formed the last working of the day back to Bala, usually from Wrexham. There were other sundry regular workings, such as the school journey from Bala to Garneddwen, and were listed in the Chester Programme.

The Central Wales workings involved were usually involved in two, three or more day circuit workings. Set 5 was a two day working and comprised five corridor coaches and worked from Birkenhead to Llangollen, returning to Ruabon and then on to Wrexham. The set was allocated to Oswestry. Set 24 was another 2 day 4 coach working and was based at Machynlleth. It worked the 12/45pm Pwllheli to Birkenhead and returned the next day with the 7.50am to Pwllheli. Set 29 was likewise a two day working, five coach set which was based at Barmouth, and worked the 7.18am to Chester and the 2/25pm back to Pwllheli. The next day it worked the 8.45am to Birkenhead and the 5/07pm back to Barmouth. Set 30 was a five coach set on a two day circuit

17. Arthog. c.1963. B.R. Standard Class 2MT engines displaced the 0-4-2T and 0-6-0PT types, for so long occupants of Penmaenpool and other 'sub' sheds. No.**78002** appears on the Dolgellau to Barmouth shuttle (which replaced the auto-coach working described previously,) which called regularly at the lonely outpost of Arthog seen with a Down train. Note the siding, and catch-point. These small locomotives were a development of the original Derby design for the L.M.S. and although initially the Western men regarded the design with some suspicion, their versatility was soon recognised by the train crews who appreciated their enclosed cab and the protection afforded by the tender extension, particularly when working bunker-first over Barmouth bridge in the depths of winter.   *Photo: C.L.Caddy.*

which was based at Wrexham. The circuit started at Birkenhead and worked the 12/25pm to Pwllheli, then the 8/15pm to Portmadoc. The next day it worked the 7.40am to Pwllheli and the 11.30am to Wrexham. It was worked as required either the same evening or the following morning to Birkenhead. Set 31 was a 3 coach set also based at Wrexham which worked daily on the 7.03am to Pwllheli and returned with the 5/25pm to Chester and then as required to Wrexham. The stock was cleaned at Pwllheli. Set 34 was a brake composite which worked, Saturdays Excepted, the 1/45pm Dolgellau to Barmouth and the 5/46pm back to Dolgellau. Set 35 was a seven coach set which worked the 11.00am Ruabon to Pwllheli on a Saturday Only, then remained in the district for the week, working circuit No.27 returning the following Saturday with the 9.20am from Barmouth to Birmingham. The stock worked back to Wrexham but details are not known. Whilst in the Central Wales District, Circuit 27 was a five day working using five coaches, two third corridor vehicles were detached and held as spare vehicles at Pwllheli during the week.

GUARDS WORKINGS

Unfortunately only one set of Guards Workings of Passenger Trains has come to light and that is for the September 1961 period. There were four duties at Bala, turns 3900-3903. Turn 3900 worked the 7.12am to Birkenhead, assist the 11.40am back to Wrexham then work the 1/05pm back to Bala. Croes

Newydd turn 3908 was a Freight Guards duty but working the 3/00pm to Morfa Mawddach before returning with a freight working. [6/45pm to Croes Newydd]. Dolgellau had turns 3915 to 3917. The first was listed as Freight Guard, and worked 2/35pm freight to Morfa Mawddach, then 5/33pm to Penrhyndeudraeth, where he changed over with Portmadoc Guard [turn 4201] and worked to Llanuwchllyn where he changed over once more with Chester London Midland Region Guard turn 74 and worked to Morfa Mawddach before returning with the 9/18pm to Dolgellau. The two remaining turns were Porter Guard workings, 3916 working the afternoon school trip from Dolgellau to Drws y Nant and back, whilst 3917 worked the morning ECS to Drws y Nant, the schools to Dolgellau and on to Barmouth with one more trip on the shuttle. Ruabon Guard turn No.3925 worked the 9.25am to Barmouth, then the 12/25pm to Penrhyndeudraeth and the 1/20pm back through to Wrexham. A Wrexham General Guard worked turn 4037 with the 6/55am to Barmouth, 10/20am to Chester and the 1/53pm to Wrexham. Turn 4038 worked the 3/25pm to Bala and returned with the 5/40pm. Barmouth Guard turn 4110 on a Saturday worked one trip on the shuttle, a trip to Llwyngwril on the coast line and back, then worked to the changeover point [usually Llanuwchllyn] with the 9/40pm and back. London Midland Freight Guards at Chester Brook Lane worked turn 253, which was the 3.20am to Barmouth returning with the 7.20am back to Wrexham daily.

STATIONS ON THE LINE
RUABON

Ruabon was the nominal terminus for passenger workings, although some regular trains did commence and terminate at Wrexham, Chester or Birkenhead. The passenger duties which started from or terminated at Ruabon usually used the bay platform which was 611 feet in length and located on the Down side. Freight trains commenced/terminated their work in the goods yard on the Down side south of the station. Trains for the Llangollen line worked south towards Shrewsbury for about 400 yards as far as Llangollen Line Junction signalbox where the line branched off on the Down side.

Ruabon was an extremely busy junction 53 miles from Oxley North between Wolverhampton and Chester. The complex was lengthy and controlled by five signalboxes with the southern most box being at Llangollen Line Junction. Alterations and developments at Ruabon South Signal Box resulted in Llangollen Line Junction box being taken out of service some time before the Barmouth line closed. The junction of the branch and the Main [Shrewsbury] line was on the Down side formed with a trailing junction. Working north, next came Ruabon South box, also on the Down side and which controlled access to the sidings complex with eight roads on the Up side of the main line. Then came Ruabon Middle box, located on the Up side and which controlled the station platform roads as well as the Goods shed, Warehouse and Down side sidings together with the loco turntable road. The turntable itself was 65 ft in diameter. North of the station on the Up side was

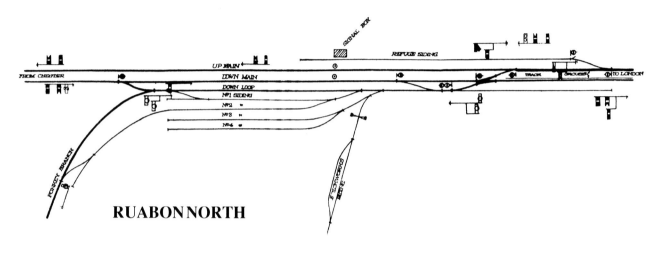

RUABON NORTH

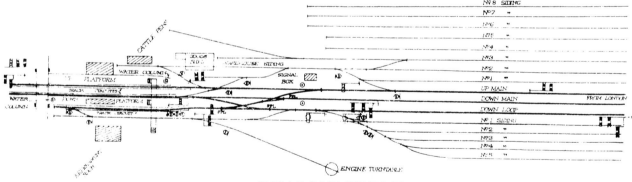

RUABON MIDDLE

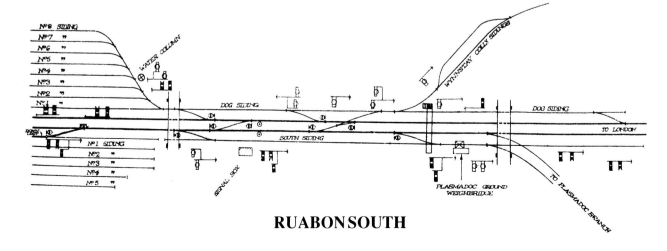

RUABON SOUTH

18. **Ruabon. 19th July 1963.** The north end of Ruabon Station was spanned by an overbridge carrying the B5097 road to Wynne Hall. Through the arch, on the Up side of the curve is Ruabon North Signal Box. The main line signal on the two-doll bracket is cleared for the departure of No.**6958** *Oxburgh Hall*, with the 12/10pm ex Paddington, for Chester and Birkenhead Woodside. The passengers in an immaculate coach No.W 34761 are interested in the activities of the photogapher, who is focussing on the early form of BR logo, still displayed on the engine's tender. Comparing this picture with subsequent photographs it will be noted that the old gas lamps which remained for so long alongside the electrical fittings have been removed. *Photo: Peter E. Baughan.*

19. **Ruabon. 19th July 1963.**0-6-0PT No.**3789** of the 5700 Class, carrying 89B [Croes Newydd] shed-code plate, enters Ruabon in the summer of 1963, with the 4/00pm Wrexham General to Bala train. In all, 863 engines of this class built in various versions of C.B.Collett's design were produced, from 1929 onwards. No.3789 was one of a slightly heavier batch, No.s 3600 - 3799, appearing from 1933 onwards, with detail alterations and a modified cab. The station is well kept. The buffer stops of the bay line are visible, across the litter free island platform, against the bridge abutment. On the Down side, the station nameboard is mounted between a pair of standard concrete posts. A series of holes drilled in the length of the 5" square posts catering for differing sizes of backboard. At the platform end is a B.R. enamelled sign bearing the legend
"PASSENGERS MUST NOT CROSS THE LINE EXCEPT BY THE FOOTBRIDGE."
Photo: Peter E.Baughan.

Ruabon North box which controlled Brickworks siding, the Down Loop, the Ponkey branch and Down side sidings. Finally came Vauxhall Colliery Box on the Up side, whose function was self explanatory.

There were several large firms who made extensive use of the railways for transporting their products, the principal ones being:

Ruabon Coal & Coke Company, Ltd.
(Hafod Collieries)
Vauxhall Colliery Company Ltd.
Wynnstay Colliery Company Ltd.
Ruabon Brick & Terra Cotta Company Ltd.,
Wyndham & Phillips Ltd. Delph Works.
The North Wales Brick & Tile Company Ltd.

All the above firms had private sidings. The Wynnstay Colliery Company worked the Plasmadoc branch to their colliery yard. The South End Up side sidings had a capacity of 201 wagons and

63 on the Down side. Ruabon Middle could store 1 wagon in the Horse Landing and 2 in the little Table Road, together with 6 wagons in the Cattle Landing, 11 in the Stable Road, 13 in the Crane Road, whilst 12 wagons inside the warehouse could be stored along with a further five outside, making a total of 50 wagons. A further 237 vehicles found accommodation on the Down side. The Refuge siding at Ruabon North on the Up side could store 37 wagons with a further 158 wagons in the Down side sidings. The density of freight traffic was such that shunting locomotives were on duty for 121 hours a week in 1947, from 1.30am until 11.00am daily apart from Sundays, and then from 2/00pm until 1.00am the next morning, in total about twenty hours daily. Some Croes Newydd footplate turns started or finished duty at Ruabon.

The main buildings were located on the Up side platform, where the Station Master had his offices. These comprised of the following:

20. Ruabon. 31st May 1963. Wearing the Class C headlamp code: one on the right of, the other in the centre on the buffer beam, and early morning (6.20am) visitor to Ruabon's Bay Platform is No. **6922**, *Burton Hall* with a van train. The train is signalled under the Signal Box Standard Bell Code Regulations of 1960 as 3 pause 1 pause 1. The full designation: "Parcels, fish, fruit, horse, livestock, meat, milk, pigeon or perishable train, composed entirely of vehicles conforming to coaching stock requirements".The building on the extreme right formerly housed the old refreshment rooms and access was by means of the footbridge. None of the day staff have yet come on duty, the gates to the station yard (left) being firmly closed.
Photo: Peter E. Baughan.

21. Ruabon. August 1954. Apart from the change in colour schemes, and installation of electric lighting, the Ruabon of 1963 differed little from that seen here. This aspect is looking south from the Up Platform, towards Ruabon Middle Signal Box which controlled the platform roads as well as the Goods Shed, Warehouse, Down Sidings and Turntable Road, with its 65 ft. diameter table. The platform seating is of regulation pattern, with two plank seats and pine back rests mounted on three cast iron stands, complete with the G.W.R. monogram design. There is a good display of contemporary posters, especially the enamelled "TANGYE PUMPS" and "VIROL" signs which must have been old even at this period.
Photo:R.E.G.Read.
Courtesy G.Biddle.

Up Side:

    Station Masters Office,
    Inspectors Office,
    Booking & Telegraph Office,
    Parcels Office (including a letter sorting office),
    First Class Ladies Waiting Room,
    Third Class Ladies Waiting Room,
    Gentlemens W.C.
    Porters Room,
    Urinals.
    Stores Hut (by the footbridge).

Down Side:

    General Waiting Room,
    Gentlemens W.C. & urinals,
    Ladies Waiting Room,
    Refreshment Room (GWR managed)
    Refreshment Rooms.
       (privately managed, GWR owned)

The Up platform is 502 feet and the Down platform 628 feet in length and remain to this day, although the Down platform is devoid of any buildings. The footbridge has lost its cover and the Up platform, although fully restored privately, has lost its canopy. Passengers have to make do with a rudimentary shelter north of the existing buildings.

The Station Master had a house on the site. There was a Truck weighbridge located at Plasmadoc Siding and a cart weighbridge in the Goods Yard, the property of a Mr. Dennis, who was bound by agreement to weigh all railway vehicles free. The crane in the goods yard had a lifting capacity of 6 tons. There was stable accommodation for six horses in the goods yard. In 1924 a Company owned lorry operated from the yard.

A water tank, holding 37000 gallons was fixed on the Down side near the south end of the platform and supplied five columns; at the Down Main platform, Up Main platform, Down sidings near Middle box, Down sidings near Bay line and in the Up siding at South end.

The Up and Down main lines, and the Bay platform line were track circuited with indicators located in Ruabon Middle box.

In 1924 there were 62 staff employed at the station, the goods yard and the five signal boxes. Additionally there was Refreshment Room staff. It was reported that at the turn of the Century the total numbers employed at Ruabon exceeded one hundred in all departments.

Dukedogs Nos **9017** and **9021** are about to leave Ruabon for Portmadoc with the Festiniog Railway Society AGM special on 26th April 1958. Note the Station Master taking charge on the platform! Festiniog AGM meetings always ensured interesting haulage for the society train over the Llangollen line, and when this route was eventually closed, over the Shrewsbury to Portmadoc section along the Cambrian Coast Line.

D. J. Lowe Archive

No.**7801** 'Anthony Manor' and Mogul No.**7314** wait by Ruabon Middle Signal Box for the arrival of the Talyllyn Railway Preservation Society's special train for the coast *via* Llangollen, on 29th Sept. 1962.

D. J. Lowe Archive

A report in the Wrexham Leader newspaper in 1986 stated that in the 1880s the Great Western Railway produced proposals to create a large workshop complex in which to build and maintain their locomotives. According to the reporter the plan was abandoned when terms could not be agreed with Sir Watkin Williams Wynn on whose land the works were to be built. Despite searches little information has yet come to light on this issue.

With the decline of the Coal Industry the importance of the goods yard declined, surviving until the early 1970s when the remaining sidings were taken out. Prior to the closure of the Barmouth line to passenger traffic, Llangollen Line Junction box was closed and removed, access to the branch controlled from Ruabon South. This box together with Ruabon North and Vauxhall Colliery Box were also closed and removed leaving Ruabon Middle Signal Box as the sole survivor. It remained manned until the early 1970s when it too became redundant. The frame controlling a crossover and signals remained until 1987 when the frame was acquired by the Llangollen Railway Society Ltd and installed in their Goods Line Junction box. The remnants of the box were demolished, although some materials were also acquired for further use at Llangollen.

22. Ruabon. 19th July 1963. L.M.S. built Jubilee 6P 4-6-0 No. **45660** *Rooke* makes an imposing entry into Ruabon with the 5/10pm train from Chester General to Paddington. On the Down Platform, a well laden parcels trolley has been parked to await the arrival of the next train. The protruding awning on the Up side displays both the method of glazing and the technique for repairing cracked panes. However, that at the apex seems to need complete renewal. *Photo: Peter E.Baughan.*

23. Ruabon. August 1960. Looking north on an unseasonable day during high summer. In this view the bay is to the left of the picture, whilst to the extreme right we have the cattle pens and dock siding. On Platform 2 a standard G.W. four-wheeled trolley is beneath the awning and it should be noted that electric lighting has been installed whilst the gas fittings are still in place. Beneath the Up side awning, a figure bends over a wicker pigeon basket. Observe also the platform awnings, that on the left spanning the island platform has glazed hipped ends. *Photo: G.H.Platt.*

24. Ruabon. August 1960. This view, facing south and taken from the footbridge shows Ruabon Middle Signal Box to the left centre, together with the eight Up and five Down sidings which were still in constant use. The sharply curved line on the extreme right leads to the turntable. The goods warehouse is in the left foreground, a chequered "restricted width" sign fixed to the door jamb. The siding passes through the building, which contained a road/rail loading dock and emerging, made a trailing connection with that seen in the foreground, leaving the Up main near the sleeper crossing. The spur then continued behind, and parallel to, the back of the Up platform to the cattle pens and dock, which were on the right, to terminate at a buffer stop. *Photo: G.H.Platt.*

25. (right) **Ruabon. 19th July 1963.** In 1924, Mr. Collett introduced the 56XX Class of 0-6-2T especially for work in the Welsh Valleys. Three years later, starting with 6600, detail alterations were made to the design. No.**6674** of Croes Newydd (89B), has eased a lengthy class K loose-coupled freight down the 1 in 75 and 1 in 314 falling gradients from Ruabon South proceeding cautiously on the Down main line. No.6674 carries a toe head-lamp on the left hand side of the buffer beam which indicates the train classifi-cation, e.g. "Freight, mineral or ballast train stopping at intermediate sta-tions. Note the three-doll, lattice girder signal bracket and the shunting signal with route indicator.

Photo: Peter E. Baughan.

26. (below) **Ruabon. 5th July 1952.** 'County' Class 4-6-0 No. **1018** *County of Leicester* climbs the bank from Cefn viaduct, past Llangollen Line Junction beyond the overbridge in the dip, and coasts past Ruabon South signal box before running into Ruabon station with a Class "B" local working to Chester. The Plasmadoc branch siding can be seen trailing right opposite the signal box. Note the close up of the back-plate fittings of the signal lamp and the spectacle plates, also the safety platform and access ladder.
Photo: T.Lewis.

No. **7827** 'Lydham Manor' is carrying the 'Talyllyn Railway Preservation Society' headboard, and accompanied by 2-6-2T No. **4555**, are seen leaving Ruabon with the AGM Special for Towyn on 26th September 1964. This was a regular yearly occurrence, dating from the inception of the 'reborn' Talyllyn Railway in the 1950's and each year utilising something varied in terms of locomotive haulage. This would be the last time the society would be able to make use of this line pending closure, requiring access to Towyn via the Shrewsbury-Pwllheli line for subsequent yearly meetings.

D. J. Lowe Archive

27. Ruabon. 28th August 1955. Near Ruabon, the old and the new on the former Great Western Chester to Shrewsbury main line. No.**73013**, allocated to Shrewsbury (84G) shed, hurries along with the Birkenhead to Paddington express towards Llangollen Line Junction. The train is passing on the left of the picture, the Plasmadoc Branch with its associated sidings and buildings. Note the Matisa Tamping Machine which stands on the 'Dog' Siding' possibly waiting for the exit signal (the lower doll) to be lowered after the passage of the express. To the left of the distinctively G.W.R. bracket signal and on the Up side can be seen the signal post relating to the Plasmadoc siding and bearing a diverse collection of shunting signals.   *Photo: T.Lewis.*

28. Ruabon. c.1955. Heading north, 2-8-0 No.**3815** pounds away with a Class D partly fitted freight near the site of Wynnstay Colliery Sidings. The engine exemplifies this powerful and versatile class. A long-lived design introduced by Mr. Churchward in 1903. No.3815 was one of a modified design brought out by Mr. Collett in 1938 with a side window cab and other minor alterations. Queen Victoria visited Wrexham and the Wynnstay Colliery during her only visit to Wales in 1889 when Princesses Beatrice and Alex, and Prince Henry descended into the mine. *Photo: T.Lewis.*

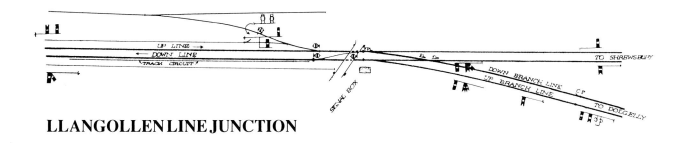

LLANGOLLEN LINE JUNCTION

29. Llangollen Line Junction. c.1955. It was the 23rd August 1889 when the Royal Train, having travelled all the way from Gosport in Hampshire, at 20 mph rumbled past a ceremonial party on Chirk Viaduct, marking the "Gateway to Wales" Apart from doubling of the line to Llangollen Goods Junction in 1900 the junction would still be recognisable to travellers from the past and we see a grimy Class 5 No.**45184** carrying Express Passenger Train headlamps crossing the junction with a Chester bound train. *Photos: E.N.Kneale.*

30. Llangollen Line Junction. c.1955. A signal box with the name Llangollen Line Junction stood for several years close to the Wynnstay overbridge but control was passed to Ruabon South Signal Box which was on the Down side. Note the tall signals with track circuit signs.

RUABON TO ACREFAIR

From Llangollen Line Junction, which is 54 chains South of Ruabon Station, the line was double for the five miles 72 chains as far as Llangollen Goods Junction Signal Box and worked under Double Line Absolute Block Regulations. Originally it was built as a single line but was doubled in 1898. The line rose on a gradient of 1 in 75 towards Acrefair some 66 chains from the junction. The line climbed on an embankment and crossed over a minor road before entering a short tunnel and the a deep cutting just before the station where the gradient levelled out.

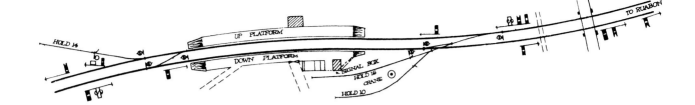

ACREFAIR

ACREFAIR

Acrefair station was built on an embankment. At this point the line passed over the Pontcysyllte mineral branch from Trevor station to Rhos which passing under the platforms.

The station buildings were of brick, and comprised a General Waiting Room and urinals on the Up side, with a Booking Office, Goods Office, General Waiting Room, a Ladies Waiting Room and two lavatories on the Down side. Siding accommodation on the Up side provided for 21 wagons on two roads, whilst the Down side could store 25 wagons, also on two roads. There was a signalbox on the Down platform, and two crossovers. In 1924, there were eight staff working the station with the Station Master rated at Class 2. Receipts particularly for Goods traffic, were good.

31. Acrefair. c.1960. A westward facing view of Acrefair taken from the spindly height of the Coed Richard footbridge which spanned the cutting. The station layout is seen to advantage, and details can be noted. Note the hip-roofed signal box, installed at the turn of the century which was of a standard pattern with a twenty-seven lever frame.

Photo: Authors Collection.

32. Acrefair. 31st May 1963. Nineteenth century Wales was mainly Non-Conformist, but had links with Pre-Reformation times. The name "Acrefair" means "The Acre of St Mary" and recalls days when an acre of land would be dedicated to the Virgin May and given to a Monastery for its use. At 7.00am on this May morning, with the Down sidings all but full, Acrefair seems secure in past and future. With the exception of the private sidings it would be closed to goods traffic on 2nd November 1964. The gradients necessitated catch points, those in the Up line being 350 yards in rear of the Up Home signal, and in the Down line, 600 yards in rear of the Down Home signal. Re-railing ramps were kept in the yard behind the signal cabin.

Photo: Peter E. Baughan.

33. Acrefair. 31st May 1963. 4-6-0 Class 4MT No.**75021**, fussily enters Acrefair with the 7.17am Class B train from Ruabon to Barmouth. The platforms were still gas-lit and on the Down side a cast iron post - identified as a No.1. type - supports an elegantly traceried "half-harp" shaped bracket with an eighteen-inch suspension, and ornate lamp controlled by a chain-pull with stamped metal "on" and "off" tags. However, the siding was equipped with electric lighting, albeit on timber posts, and we can observe the light fittings above the stabled vans. Passengers at Acrefair utilized a barrow crossing and B.R. enamelled sins at the foot of the platform ramps bleakly warn "BEWARE OF THE TRAINS". The platform awnings are similar to those we shall examine in detail at other stations and also note the manner in which conscientious staff placed the sack trucks out of harm's way.

Photo: Peter E.Baughan.

34. Trevor. c.1950. A view facing west through Trevor from the road overbridge. The Down sidings are quite full with a group of flat wagons carrying palletised loads of bricks from McGinnis's Siding, whose works are out of sight on the extreme right but reached by the siding branching off to the rear of the signal box. Other stock comprises an 'XP' fitted van, a chemical tanker and empty sheet wagon, with side doors open, ready for loading from a carrier's cart. At the end of the siding near the water tank, and attached to a rake of mineral wagons, is a similar wagon, with the 'sheet rail' in the raised position and the tented tarpaulin fitted and roped down. The signal in the right corner is No.29. (Up Starter), and note the barrier placed to prevent passengers crossing the line at this end of the station.

Photo: Speed Publications.

35. Trevor. c.1950. Framed by the Weighbridge, Water Tank, and Down starter Signal (No.2.) the 0-6-0 Pannier Tank which has worked the 6.34am freight from Ruabon Yard placidly shunts the sidings. Average Point to Point Allowances for such trains were, Ruabon to Ruabon South, 2 mins., Ruabon South to Acrefair 3 mins., Acrefair to Trevor 3 mins. On the return trip however the timings were Trevor to Acrefair 4 mins., Acrefair to Stop Board 1 min., Stop Board to Ruabon South 4 mins., and to Ruabon 3 mins. In the yard are more of the sheet wagons, in demand for traffic from Monsanto Chemical Works which also had its own sidings. In the distance are the Llangollen end sidings, with a rake of pallett wagons and 'fitted' vans deposited by the engine. Note the 'unclimable' wrought iron fencing to the rear of the platform.

Photo: Speed Publications.

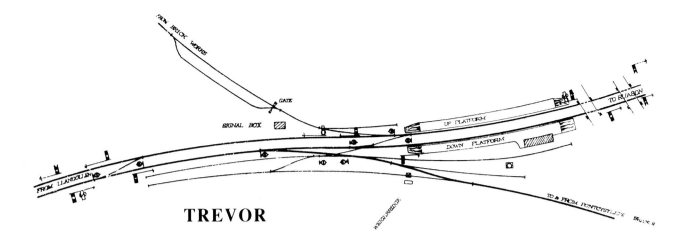

TREVOR

ACREFAIR TO TREVOR

The gradient fell at 1 in 85 after leaving Acrefair station, which ensured that Up trains kept steam on until they reached the change of grade. The line then crossed over the main Llangollen to Ruabon road on a high skew arch bridge before entering a cutting. The terrain altered greatly, the line changing from cutting to embankment frequently. It also swung through ninety degrees on the 78 chain section to Trevor.

TREVOR

The line entered Trevor station under a bridge carrying the Llangollen to Ruabon road. The station was very important, being located in the industrial area of the Dee valley, at a distance of 1 mile 64 chains from Llangollen Line Junction. Close by is the aqueduct carrying the Shropshire Union Canal over the Dee valley. Passenger trains generally took eight minutes to travel from Ruabon. There was a pillar tank located in the goods yard which was on the Down side. On the Up side at the Llangollen end was a 32 lever signalbox.

The station buildings, which were of brick construction, comprised One General Waiting Room on the Up Side, whilst the Down platform accommodation consisted of a Booking Office, Parcels Office, General Waiting Room, Ladies Waiting Room, a Lamp Room and Small Warehouse built of corrugated

sheet, and two lavatories. The three sidings at the Acrefair end of the yard held 64 wagons, whilst the two at the Llangollen end held 32.

The Pontcysyllte branch ran back out of the goods yard towards Ruabon. On the Up side a private siding from Roberts & McGinnis's Brick Works connected with the main line near the signal box.

In 1924 there were five staff working at the station consisting of one clerk, two signalmen and two leading porters. The Station Master at Acrefair supervised the running of the station and goods yard.

Traffic from Trevor was always heavy, and the Pontcysyllte branch was very difficult to work. This mineral branch was a single line, three miles 67 chains in length and divided into two sections namely:

Trevor to Cefn Crossing
Cefn Crossing to Rhos (Brook Street)

Each section was worked with a wooden train staff and One Engine in Steam operation prevailed. The gates were padlocked across the line and attended to by the guard working the branch. Apart from the initial falling gradient out of Trevor goods yard over Station Road level crossing, the line climbed almost all the way to Rhos.

36. Trevor. c.1950. Near to the weighbridge office at Trevor, amongst a clutter of disused equipment, was a massive hand-grindstone, nowadays an eminently collectable and sought after item. The yard is cleared of most traffic apart from the ubiquitous sheet-wagons. The sheeting of any loaded wagons, whether fitted with central tent bars or not, was important, not only for weather protection, but, particularly in the case of inflammables or explosives, to reduce fire risks from sparks thrown out by the engine. Comprehensive procedures were detailed in rules, such as No.s. 131, 173 and 240 (10). Yard-masters jealously guarded their stocks and if things got desperate one of the stock Telegraphic Messages was "COVMAND" Heavy demand for sheets. *Photo: Speed Publications.*

37. **Trevor. 7th November 1960.** Leaving Trevor at 9.36am with the 9.31am Ruabon to Barnouth Class B train is 2-6-0 No.**6357**. The signal box was one of a number installed circa. 1895/1900 and replacing a rather rudimentary installation dating from two decades earlier. The new structure, brick-framed, measured 25 ft. x 12 ft., and had a hipped, slate-hung roof. It was fitted with a G.W.R. Double-Twist locking frame. The signal standing in the V between the Up line and siding was operated by lever No.30. The Pontcysyllte Branch could be accessed via the crossover and slip in front of No.**6357**.
Photo: Norman Jones.

38. (Centre) **Trevor.** Taken from the Down platform looking towards Ruabon, this view shows the main station buildings on the Up side with the main Llangollen to Ruabon road passing over the tracks on a stone built skew arch bridge. The goods yard is adjacent to the Up platform, although there is little sign of activity with the yard crane standing motionless. The Pontcysyllte branch passes between the trees on the right of the picture and falls away sharply.
Photo: Speed Publications.

39. (Below) **Trevor. 1964.** A retrospective view of the goods yard taken from a Barmouth train. Notice the parachute water tank in the yard and beyond that the weighbridge hut. At the foot of the trees can just be seen the gate which marked the boundary and commencement of the Pontcysyllte branch.
Photo: G.H.Platt.

TREVOR TO LLANGOLLEN [GOODS LINE JUNCTION]

On leaving Trevor the line falls at 1 in 75 towards Sun Bank Halt before levelling out and then varying to 1 in 110 rising. The section from Trevor to Llangollen is three and a half miles.

Wrights Siding was just over a mile on from Trevor and was put in to accommodate traffic from the lime rocks quarried nearby. At one time the siding was controlled by a signal box, but this was removed between the wars when the siding was taken out.

SUN BANK HALT

Half a mile beyond Wrights Siding was Sun Bank Halt, a stopping place which consisted of wooden platforms on each side of the line, each with a corrugated iron shelter. The halt was rarely used and no staff were employed there. Tickets were issued and collected by guards of the few trains that called. During the winter months the care and control of the platform lamps was the responsibility of the Corwen District Inspector. In September 1945, a fatal accident occurred to the early morning Mail train, when the Shropshire Union Canal burst its banks, the water draining away and washing out the track bed and ballast leaving the sleepered rails suspended in mid air. Unfortunately the telephone circuit was not affected and the first train of the day entered the section from Trevor to Llangollen Goods Line

Junction unaware of the disaster. The train plunged down the embankment killing the driver and setting fire to the wagons. The military were called in to assist in the recovery and effect repairs, but the difficult location prevented the recovery of the locomotive, 2-6-0 No. 6315 which was cut up on the spot.

Before reaching Llangollen Station, Factory Crossing appeared where a private road to a woollen factory crossed the line, protected by gates that were normally locked across the roadway. A porter was sent from Llangollen with the key to open the gates when necessary and a telephone was provided at the crossing. The key for the gates was normally kept in Llangollen station signal box.

40. Sun Bank. 8th September 1945. A view from above the track showing the extent of the washout and the flooding on the fields caused by the washout. The 45 ton rail mounted crane was worked over the Rhyl-Denbigh-Corwen line and forward to the site. Most of the wreckage caught fire.   *Photo: National Museum of Wales. Neg:BB/415/35*

41. Sun Bank. 7th September 1945. Shows a view of the tangled wreckage of the 3.35am Mails and Goods train from Chester to Barmouth, which was worked as a Class F train, hauled by 2-6-0 No.**6315** and comprised two bogie vans and 14 4-wheeled wagons and a 20-ton brake van ran into a breach in the track, caused by the canal having burst its banks. *Photo: National Museum of Wales. Neg:BB/415/34.*

42. Sun Bank. 18th September 1945. Filling in operations by the Military and Railway Staff. The locomotive was not recoverable and was cut up on site. The line was reopened for traffic fifteen days later. Unfortunately Driver D.Jones was killed but the Fireman and Guard survived.
Photo: National Museum of Wales. Neg: BB/416/2.

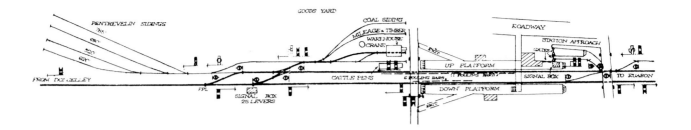

LLANGOLLEN

Located five and a half miles from Llangollen Line Junction, the town was and still is the main attraction for tourists to the Dee valley and over the years created much of the traffic over the line. In the period between the two world wars excursion trains from Liverpool ran every Sunday and were well patronised. The station is a dominant feature of the town, situated alongside the River Dee, a fact which restricted development over the years. Access to the station is by a private road leading off the bridge and Abbey Road on the Up side, where the main buildings are located at platform level. When the line opened, there was a single platform on the Up side but not at the present location. The construction of the Llangollen and Corwen Railway included the building of a new station on the present site.

Subsequent improvements when the line was doubled from Ruabon included providing a Down platform on the river side of the site and lengthening of the Up platform, the two platforms being connected by a passenger footbridge the end of which overhangs the river. At the foot of the ramp, the tracks were crossed by the usual type of trolley path constructed with longitudinal timbers in the 'four' and 'six' foot. The station site has physical restrictions, both platforms being extremely long and forming an elongated "S" configuration.

The main buildings, which are constructed of brick, contained a combined General Waiting Room and Booking Hall, Booking Office, Ladies Waiting Room, Parcels Office, Porters Room and two lavatories. On the Up platform but east of the

43. Llangollen. c.1957. Beside a River Dee with levels depleted by a hot summer, and under Bowling Green footbridge, some 5m 20ch from Llangollen Line Junction, comes old friend No.**6357**, whose footplate was very familiar to one of the authors in those halcyon years. Always a free steamer she is blowing off slightly and one can imagine the squeal of the wheels pressing against the check rails on the reverse curves nearing Bishop Trevor's fine bridge, and Llangollen station. The catch point is a notable feature of the Up siding, and some engineering work is in hand, as witness the temporary lighting units wired up adjacent to the river wall to the right of 6357.   *Photo: J.W.T.House, C.L.Caddy Collection.*

44. Llangollen. c.1953. This idyllic shot encapsules the image of a Llangollen relaxing after the rigours of World War II, but not yet overtaken by the motor car invasion. In the quiet streets, with absolutely no parking problems, is a jolly two-seater, with a rumble seat and canvas hood. Passing the station approach is a horse and trap whilst further on is a Morris '8' creating quite a 'dash' in comparison to its companions. The signal box on the platform is switched out, the signals on their tall wooden posts resting at "clear". However, the permanent way gang have been fettling the track judging by the amount of new ballast in evidence, no doubt a Sunday job. In those days there was very little "bussing", usually going in trains composed of ancient stock, or sometimes brake vans, and came back the same way.
Photo: P.E.Baughan collection.

main building is Llangollen Station Signalbox which contains a frame of 25 levers. At the time of the lines closure, 11 levers were spare. Even back in 1924 the box was not regularly manned but opened for traffic purposes as required. Three track circuits were provided to the running lines. A short siding to a horse landing extends behind the signalbox and at one time a loading gauge was located here. Cattle traffic was occasionally handled here. The siding could accommodate four wagons and access is by trailing connection controlled by the Station signalbox. Another siding off the Up line beyond the road overbridge this time made with a facing connection could accommodate five wagons. This was taken out of use some time before the lines' closure.

The Corwen end of the Up platform contains a separate building which housed a General Waiting Room and a Ladies Waiting Room. This section was called the Excursion Platform but in reality an extension to the main Up platform face. There are separate ramps to both platforms which enable passengers to gain access from Church Road which crosses the line by the Goods Shed. Both ramps are gated, and excursion trains disgorged or entrained their passengers at this end of the station and which could be scrutinised by station staff.

The Down platform has a small brick structure which contained a General Waiting Room, Ladies Waiting Room and two lavatories. A large water tank stood back from and overlooked the Down platform and supplied water to three columns, two on the Down platform at the Corwen end, and one on the Up platform at the Ruabon end. The column was located on the ramp.

The station staff in 1924 comprised a Stationmaster [Class 2], Goods Clerk, Booking Clerk, Junior Clerk, 2 signalmen [at Goods Junction box], 1 porter signalman, who looked after Station signalbox, 1 Ticket Collector, 1 Checker, 1 Parcels Porter, 1 Goods Porter, 3 Porters and a Waiting Room

Attendant. One porter relieved at Berwyn station for four hours daily. Also in 1924, the G.W.R. provided a bus between Corwen and Llangollen on Sundays, and there was considerable road competition from the Wrexham & District Transport and Crosville Motor Company [the predecessor to Crosville Motor Services Ltd] Not to be out-done, according to the tourist literature, the Shropshire Union Canal also competed for heavy traffic!

INTERNATIONAL EISTEDDFOD
AT
LLANGOLLEN
WEDNESDAY, 6th JULY, 1960

Second Class Day Excursion Fare	Depart At		Arrival Time on Return
s. d. 12/-	a. m. 9-00	LLANDUDNO	p. m. 8-00
11/6	9-05	DEGANWY	7-55
11/3	9-10	LLANDUDNO JUNCTION	7-50
10/6	9-15	COLWYN BAY	7-40
9/3	9-30	ABERGELE	7-30
7/3	9-55	FLINT	6-55
6/6	10-00	CONNAHS QUAY	6.50
6/3	10-05	SHOTTON LOW LEVEL	6-45
5/-	10-20	CHESTER GENERAL	6-25
	a. m. 11-15	arrive LLANGOLLEN depart	p. m. 5-30

Children under three years of age, free ; three years and under fourteen, half-fare.

Further information will be supplied on application to Stations, Official Railway Agents, or to H. W. T. YOUNG, District Traffic Superintendent, Chester. [Tel. Chester 24680, Ext. 28).

Travel in Rail Comfort

June 1960   B.R. 35000

F. 298   **LONDON MIDLAND**

Hugh Evans & Sons Ltd, L'pool

Croes Newydd based 16XX 0-6-0PT No.**1660**, seen from the main road over bridge at Llangollen, is involved in a shunting procedure with a brake van. Croes Newydd MPD had several of these Pannier Tanks on their books which serviced similar duties on the Llangollen line, although the 57XX and 74XX varieties were more commonly observed. This July 1956 scene would have been at the height of the busy holiday period on the railway, and such operations would have had to have been performed quickly and efficiently in order not to delay passenger rail traffic to and from the coast.

D. J. Lowe Archive

74xx 0-6-0PT No.**7431** with a local Bala to Ruabon passenger service in Llangollen station in 1954. The close proximity of the River Dee to the railway at this point is very evident. *D. J. Lowe Archive*

Chester based ex GWR 51xx 2-6-2T No.**5179** at Llangollen with an Eisteddfod 'shuttle' passenger train for Chester during the summer of 1957. It was common practise at this time for Chester based 51xx tank engines to be used on these shuttles, and they would run between Chester and Llangollen during Eisteddfod week. The first shuttle however would see the 51xx class loco departing Bala (Town) at 7.12am for Birkenhead, (the loco having worked down to Bala the previous day on the 9.20pm Chester to Bala passenger train, arriving 11.05pm and staying overnight at Bala loco depot). Other shuttles ran during the day, the last one being the 4.20pm Chester to Llangollen (arr.5.19pm), returning 5.35pm from Llangollen and arriving back at Chester at 6.49pm. *D. J. Lowe Archive*

A very grimy looking, and typical of the times, BR Standard Class 4 4-6-0 No.**75026** with the 12.45pm Pwllhelli-Chester passenger service, calls at Llangollen on 11th April 1964. The Cleveland Petrol station on the main road has a fine array of pumps to cater for the demand from the increasing motor car competition.

D. J. Lowe Archive

A view taken from the southern side of the River Dee sees 53XX Class Mogul No.**5399** running tender first with an ordinary passenger train. The Eisteddfod was also held during July of this year (1956) and it is quite possible we see **5399** being pressed into helping out with the Eisteddfod shuttles, (Chester-Llangollen-Chester). Having disgorged its passengers, the returning stock doesn't appear to be carrying many passengers, if any, judging by the lack of people in the leading coach. There being no turntable at Llangollen forfeits No.**5399** the privilege of running chimney first! .

D. J. Lowe Archive

45. (left) **Llangollen. c.1955.** Another delightfully atmospheric shot of a period Llangollen, the G.W.R. pattern name-board complemented by an elegant gas lamp interesting in that it appears to have been adapted from a "full Harp" bracket fitting. There was no automatic ignition nor were operating chains fitted, so it is assumed that a lamplighter would be on the duty roster, in hours of darkness of course. A special tool for this job comprised a long pole fitted near the top with a hook which could be inserted beneath the flap into the housing where engagement with a hole in the keyed tap would enable the supply to be turned on. The top of this pole fitted into the base of a round, usually brass lamp oil reservoir which was fitted with a filler and wick holder, a perforated metal casing surrounding the flame and protecting it from draught but also allowing the flow of gas through the mantle in the lamp casing to become ignited. Armed with this device which was lit in the lamp room, and a short inverted V form ladder, an array of gas lamps could be very quickly lit. Continuity however was not maintained in other aspects of rail activity. Churn traffic was declining, a fact underlined by the road motor milk tanker to the left of the bridge. Flanking it, another competitor, the splendid Bryn Melyn Motor Services coach, in its impressive white livery, with a green flash, strategically placed near the station approach. *Photo: J.H.Moss.*

46.(below) **Llangollen. 10th September 1956.** Chester (84K) engine No.**7801** *Anthony Manor*, somewhat begrimed, arrives at Llangollen at 12/21pm with train 1M07 the 10.20am Barmouth to Birkenhead. The leading vehicle is a horse-box, perpetuating a practise from the very earliest days of railways when the gentlefolk travelled accompanied by their carriages on flat trucks with their bloodstock in primitive forms of horse-van. The vehicles of the nineteen fifties were built to coaching stock requirements and were vacuum fitted, well sprung, heated and with screw couplings. From the viewpoint on the Dee bridge, we can observe the river containment walls and the ingenious cantilevering of the stringers, landings and vertical columns of the end of the unglazed footbridge over the river. *Photo: Norman Jones.*

The Double Line Signalling block section extended from Trevor to Llangollen Goods Line Junction, half a mile beyond the station, although Llangollen Station Signalbox could be switched in as required. The line rises through the station and special provision was made in the Sectional Appendix to cover this fact, causing specific conditions to be imposed with regard to shunting and attaching of vehicles within station limits.

Llangollen Goods Line Junction Signal Box was located on the Down side and marked the end of two line running from Ruabon Llangollen Line Junction and the commencement of the single line track to Barmouth Junction. To the west, the line was controlled by Single Line Token System to Glyndyfrdwy with provision for switching in and token exchange facility provided at Deeside Loop

47 (above) **Llangollen. August 1954.** The elongated layout of Llangollen was the result of circumstances rather than design, due to its location between the river Dee and Abbey Road, and so despite its private approach to the small forecourt and horse-dock, this aspect of the main buildings is, at first sight, unimpressive   *Photo: G.Biddle.*

48. (Centre) **Llangollen. September 1963.** The Up side looking west illustrates the length and sinuous curves of the platforms, and highlights the structural complexities of station awnings.   *Photo: R.E.G.Read,*
G.Biddle collection.

49. (Below) **Llangollen. July 1952.** A typical branch freight working with one of Croes Newydd 0-6-0PT trundles through Llangollen with a Bala to Ruabon Class K freight, passing the station box on the Up platform. It was 'Eisteddfod' week and the bunting adds to the festivites. A vintage Crosville Leyland Tiger Cub, formerly N33 serves as a mobile booking and tours office.   *Photo: W.G.Rear.*

Access to the goods yard at Llangollen was made at Llangollen Goods Line box on the Up side by single line off a loop road which could hold thirty wagons and ran parallel to Abbey Road before widening out into the goods yard. The yard itself, which was at a higher level than the main lines, contained a warehouse of traditional design which provided covered accommodation for four wagons, and had two small offices adjoining the building. The warehouse itself contained two cranes, each with a lifting capacity of one ton, whilst a third crane in the yard could lift five tons. The yard also contained a cart weighbridge and cattle pen accommodation with an adjacent loading bank but, as already mentioned, cattle traffic was sometimes dealt with at the passenger station. Road access to the yard was off Abbey Road. There were four sidings in the yard which could store 108 wagons, with a loading gauge where the tracks converged. At the Barmouth end of the goods loop the track ran parallel to the main line and which subsequently widened out to a nest of four sidings which could accommodate 188 wagons. However a regular function of three of the sidings was to provide stabling for excursion coaching stock. No.4. siding was extended towards the canal and at one time led to an adjoining wharf where slates were transhipped. The extension part of this siding was privately owned, and was reduced in the 1920s to the G.W.R. boundary.

50. Llangollen. c.1960. A nostalgic view of bustling Llangollen where No. **7811** *Dunley Manor,* a Croes Newydd (89B) engine, has just arrived with an express working from Barmouth, coming to a stand just clear of the smoke deflector plates on the footbridge.To the extreme right of the photograph, attached to the signal box, is an elaborate corner bracket from which is suspended a fine example of a two-mantle gas lamp. The bar regulating the supply and associated pull-wires are clearly visible. *Photo: J.H.Moss.*

51. Llangollen. 19th July 1963. An unusual west facing view from the footbridge as 57XX Class 0-6-0PT No.**3789** departs with the 4/00pm from Wrexham to Bala. Overlooking the platforms the Victorian Villas lend an air of gentility to the station. The station name totems are cantilevered from the gas lamps. *Photo: Peter E.Baughan.*

A general view of the western end of Llangollen station looking eastwards. Note the neatly attended grassy slopes by the GWR water tank and the impressive brick curved buttress walling on the left. Gently sloping pathways lead down to the platforms on each side flanked by typical wrought iron railings. "Foxcote Manor" No.**7822** can be seen making an entrance with an express service to the Cambrian Coast one day in July 1956.

D. J. Lowe Archive

52. Llangollen. c. 1960. A definitive and comprehensive eastward facing view of Llangollen, with assorted sizes of display boards on the grey stone walls, although not all of them are in use. This aspect shows the way in which the awnings were divided into two sections by the footbridge, beneath the soffit of which appear, the signal box, water crane, bracket signal - with the track circuit diamond bold on the post -and the loading gauge over the cattle dock. The house on the left has a railed balcony which would be excellent for train-spotting, although it was probably designed with river views in mind. This western end of the station buildings is finished, and the beams capped, in a similar manner to the eastern. An unusual feature of the roof at gutter level is the presence of a railing approximately two feet in height. The Down platform is punctuated by more of Llangollen's graceful lamps, whilst adjacent to the footbridge staircase is the gritting bin.

Photo: G.Biddle.

53. Llangollen. 7th November 1960. 2-6-0 No.**6357**, a Croes Newydd engine heading train 2V89, the 7.50am Birkenhead to Pwllheli, takes water at Llangollen. Regulating the flow to the tender at the water crane adjacent to the platform buildings is Fireman J.A.Jones, of Chester, who incidentally later emigrated to the Antipodes. When Inspector F.W.Wiggett and the author joined No.6357 at Ruabon, the first job was to chalk-mark the level on the tender gauge, as consumption and steaming checks were to be made. Like so many things connected with steam locomotive operation this was a simple yet effective method of obtaining vital information.

Photo: Norman Jones.

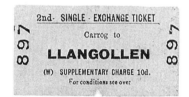

2nd- SINGLE - EXCHANGE TICKET
Carrog to
LLANGOLLEN
(W) SUPPLEMENTARY CHARGE 10d.
For conditions see over
897   897

54. Llangollen. c.1960. No.6357 was a regular visitor to Llangollen and at first sight this might appear to be the same working as in the previous photograph. It will be observed however that the coaching stock is quite different. In November 1960 there was merely the branch set of stock to which were added vans for Barmouth. In this view, a type of coach possibly of Eastern Region origin with oval lavatory windows glazed opaque opal, is leading, whilst a main line vehicle with name-boards is in the centre of the rake. From the Down platform to the right of No.6357 is the inclined ramp exit leading to Church Road, which crossed the line by an overbridge just beyond the end of the platforms. There was a corresponding exit on the Up side. We note also that the permanent way gang have been busy on the Up line spreading a layer if fresh white ballast.

Photo: C.L.Caddy.

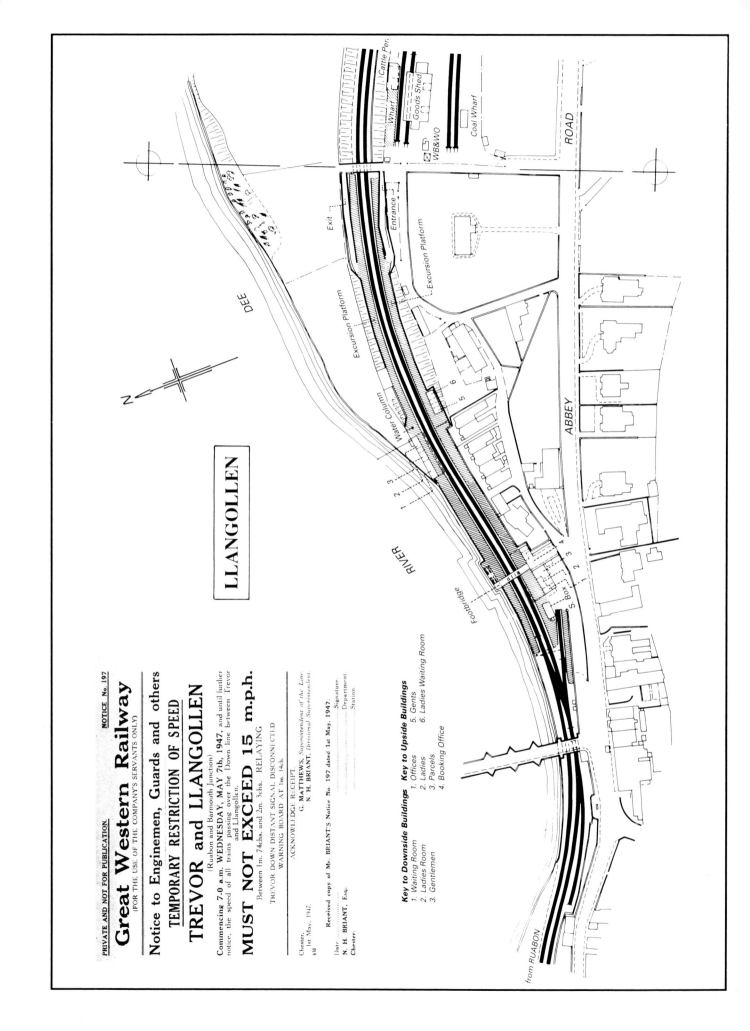

PRIVATE AND NOT FOR PUBLICATION.   NOTICE No. 197

Great Western Railway

(FOR THE USE OF THE COMPANY'S SERVANTS ONLY)

Notice to Enginemen, Guards and others
TEMPORARY RESTRICTION OF SPEED
TREVOR and LLANGOLLEN
(Ruabon and Barmouth Junction)

Commencing 7.0 a.m. **WEDNESDAY, MAY 7th, 1947,** and until further notice, the speed of all trains passing over the Down line between Trevor and Llangollen.

MUST NOT EXCEED 15 m.p.h.

Between 1m. 74chs. and 2m. 3chs. RELAYING

TREVOR DOWN DISTANT SIGNAL DISCONNECTED
WARNING BOARD AT 1m. 14ch.

ACKNOWLEDGE RECEIPT.

G. MATTHEWS, *Superintendent of the Line.*
N. H. BRIANT, *Divisional Superintendent.*

Chester,
1st May, 1947.

Received copy of Mr. BRIANT'S Notice No. 197 dated 1st May, 1947.

.................................Signature.
.................................Department.
.................................Station.

Date ....
N. H. BRIANT, Esq.
Chester.

650

Key to Downside Buildings
1. *Waiting Room*
2. *Ladies Room*
3. *Gentlemen*

Key to Upside Buildings
1. *Offices*
2. *Ladies*
3. *Parcels*
4. *Booking Office*
5. *Gents*
6. *Ladies Waiting Room*

LLANGOLLEN

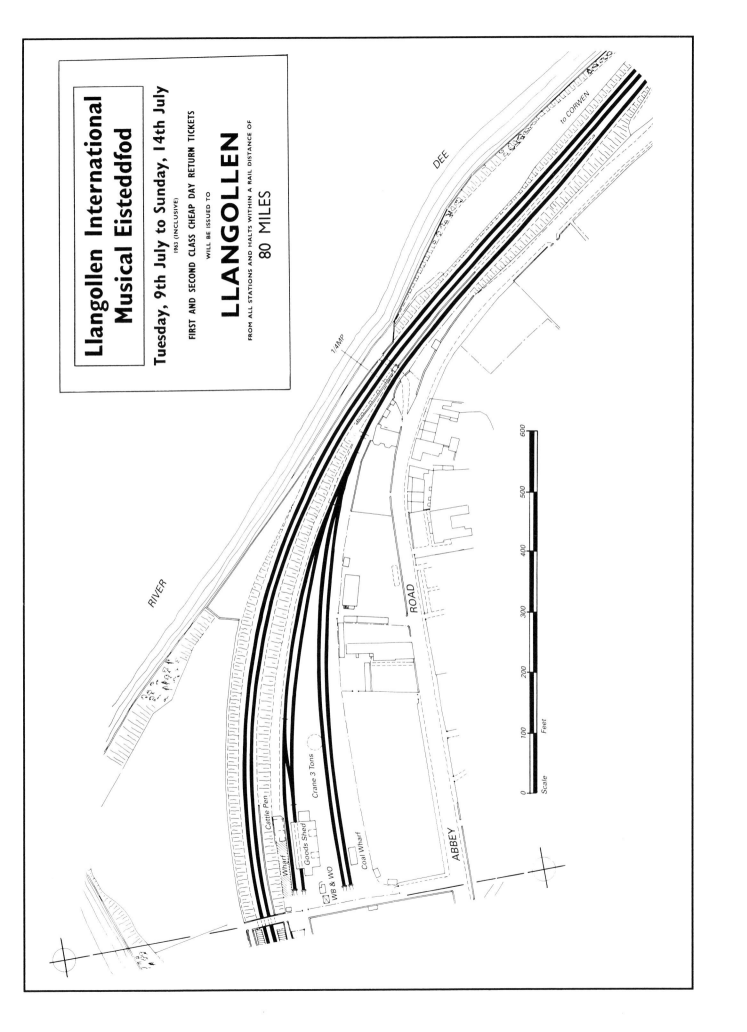

Llangollen International
Musical Eisteddfod

Tuesday, 9th July to Sunday, 14th July
1963 (INCLUSIVE)

FIRST AND SECOND CLASS CHEAP DAY RETURN TICKETS

WILL BE ISSUED TO

LLANGOLLEN

FROM ALL STATIONS AND HALTS WITHIN A RAIL DISTANCE OF

80 MILES

to CORWEN

DEE

1/4MP

RIVER

ROAD

ABBEY

Cattle Pen

Wharf

Goods Shed

Crane 3 Tons

Coal Wharf

WB & WO

Scale   Feet

0   100   200   300   400   500   600

55. Llangollen. 31st May 1963. It is noticeable that the Up line has again been receiving attention probably due to track movement as a result of the cant. Other aspects of the line have also changed in that the London Midland Region has now taken over and a British Railways standard 4MT No. **75021**, instead of a former "Western" locomotive appears on the 7.17am Ruabon to Barmouth. There were through coaches from Wrexham attached to the train at Ruabon At the end of the Down platform, in the corner of the overbridge abutment, stands the Llangollen Goods distant signal, above it the platform starter and nearby the second of the Down side water cranes. The Up side "gents" is, not surprisingly constructed of glazed bricks, whilst the neat awning is cantilevered out from the main building, without the benefit of any supporting columns. The two seats beneath the awning are standard G.W.R. issue.

Photo: Peter E. Baughan.

56. Llangollen. c.1910. An early twentieth century, yet timeless and tranquil Llangollen, drowsing beneath the ruins of Castell Dinas Bran. The river Dee, glass-smooth to the weir, becomes exuberant beneath the four pointed arches of the 14th. century bridge. The chamfered arch rings are built in two orders, and there are triangular refuges over the cut-waters between the parapets. The station was smaller but the scene would be similar, when Queen Victoria visited the area in 1889. Following the Royal visit to Wynnstay, a trip to Llangollen was planned for the afternoon by special train and as one expects, regulations for working Royal Trains were always rigorous. Road traffic was to be halted at level crossings long before the train was due, shunting was to cease thirty minutes before the special arrived, Station Masters were to be on duty, etc. etc. and a Pilot Engine was to precede the Royal Train. Over the years nothing changed much, confirmed to some degree by a London Midland and Scottish Railway Co., "Notice of Special Royal Trains London (Euston) to Edinburgh (Princes Street) on 4th/5th July 1937 was very similar in content.

Photo: Clwyd Record Office.

57. Llangollen. 19th April 1959. Once the single line is gained at Llangollen Goods Junction signal box the line climbs towards Berwyn and crosses the river Dee on a three span bridge. With Llangollen becoming a popular tourist attraction from Merseyside, regular excursion trains were run from Liverpool and the limited confines of the station site made storage of passenger stock difficult. This was remedied by constructing a nest of sidings alongside the former canal siding at Pentrefelin, where stock could be stored without congesting the platform roads and goods yard sidings. Access to the sidings was taken off the Goods yard headshunt, which was extended on the level through a gate and fanning out. Between the wars in the season, at least two trains ran every Sunday. *Photo: G.H.Platt.*

A view looking eastwards from Llangollen Goods Junction Signal Box to where the line climbs up to the goods yard, with the main running lines leading to the station on the right. Note the small shunt signal on the signal post. An early 1960's view.   *D. J. Lowe Archive*

A delightful view of Llangollen station looking eastwards. Taken from platform one. What cannot be fully appreciated is just how narrow the land available was to the early railway builders for them to construct the station. This restriction required the attractive looking footbridge to be built out over the River Dee, such that passengers walking down the steps on the right here are in fact cantilevered out over the rapid falls of the river. The station has all the charm one associates with a GWR built establishment, even in this early 1960's view.   *D. J. Lowe Archive*

No.**7817** 'Garsington Manor' approaching Llangollen with a Barmouth to Chester express, in July 1957. This particular 'Manor' was very much a regular fixture to the loco rosters for this sort of work on this line, during this period. Llangollen goods yard was located on the other side of the hedgerow above the train; access to which was via Llangollen Goods Line Junction Signal Box, about a quarter of a mile to the rear of the train.

D. J. Lowe Archive

LLANGOLLEN GOODS LINE JUNCTION TO BERWYN

Once the single line commenced, the line swung through ninety degrees as it climbed to cross the River Dee at Berwyn Bridge, a skew metal structure and one of the main engineering structures on the line. The track followed the contour of the hillside, and the combination of severe curves and a gradient of 1 in 80 imposed speed restrictions on Up trains and produced a healthy sounding exhaust from Down workings. The countryside closed in as Berwyn station was reached, just over a mile from Goods line Junction box.

BERWYN

The platform is on the Down side of the line, and the station building is an imposing structure comprising a Booking Office, General Waiting Room, a Ladies Waiting Room and two lavatories. The upper part of the building provided residential accommodation for the Station Master until that post was dispensed with. At one time, signals were provided for stopping trains who were conditionally required to call, but these were removed in the late 1920s. There was no signal cabin so they were controlled from a small open frame on the platform. As built, the platform length was quite short but was extended over the viaduct although this was removed before the line closed. There was no provision

58. Berwyn. 31st May 1963 Travelling on towards Corwen, No.**75021**, having negotiated Llangollen Goods Junction has crossed the Dee bridge on the now single line, climbed the 1 in 80 gradient through the trees above the river and slows for a call at the attractively located station of Berwyn. The platform approach for foot passengers (seen appearing ahead of 75021) was steep, and despite being terraced, could be treacherous in wet or frosty weather. A sensible feature was the placing of a safety fence at the platform end of the path, whilst a left turn was required to pass through the wicket gate into the station. *Photo: Peter E.Baughan.*

made for goods traffic, this being dealt with by Llangollen station, although the line did deal with parcels traffic. In 1924, traffic receipts totalled £614, of which £122 came from the parcels traffic. The Station Masters grade was Class 6. Traffic diminished after the second world war, and few trains were required to stop. With the development of Llangollen Railway, Berwyn assumed an important role as the western terminus of the preserved line for three years, until the extension to Deeside Loop opened in April 1990. The station will continue to enjoy a high profile in the future being a dominant landmark alongside the A5 in a particularly beautiful setting.

G.W.R.
Llangollen

59. Berwyn. Looking along the platform towards Corwen and Barmouth, this view shows the charm of the station in its surroundings. The nameboard is still in the traditional G.W.R. style, although the word "Halt" appears to have been an afterthought. The gas lamp beyond is probably unchanged after forty years. The rudimentary wooden shelter indicates that the halt has been unstaffed for some time, with perhaps only the sign affixed to the side of the shelter being modern. The seat is a period piece, and now much sought after by collectors. There is an air of neglect about the place however, and the shrubs and trees are encroaching the platform and obscuring the view of the river, the Chain Bridge and the hotel of the same name. The platform extension over the viaduct has been removed. *Photo: Speed Publications.*

No.**75021** climbs towards Berwyn Halt on 4ᵗʰ April 1964 with the 1.35pm Chester to Barmouth passenger service. This part of the line is now preserved enabling travellers to experience the same climb up to Berwyn Halt and beyond (as far as Carrog).

D. J. Lowe Archive

60. Berwyn. July 1963. A view east featuring traditional motive power at Berwyn with 57XX Class 0-6-0PT No.**3789** leaving for Bala. At this point the minor road to Ruthin, leaving the A5, makes a steep descent to pass beneath the railway. By the 1890's, thanks to Sir John Lubbock, Bank Holidays were enjoyed by the working classes and many artisans by means of "Holiday Clubs". As a result, those making regular savings could take an annual holiday. Railways of course had a near monopoly of the traffic and responded by putting on excursions and special trains to places like Llangollen, and Telfords artificial Horseshoe Falls (intended as a feeder for the canal) near Berwyn. Platforms were extended and a wooden addition - removed by the time of this picture - was provided on the south side of the viaduct. It would certainly have been invaluable for the present Llangollen Railway Society for the working of their trains. *Photo: R.E.G.Read. G.Biddle collection.*

61. Berwyn. c.1963. The London Midland Region seemed to introduce a "foreign" atmosphere into branch and secondary main line workings, and the natural use of Welsh between footplate and station staff would enhance this impression. Here, B.R. Standard Class 4MT 4-6-0 No.**75009** pulls away from rest and gets to grips with the 1 in 80 gradient and the curve across the viaduct, blasting steam from the cylinder drain cocks which obliterate the view in front of the train. The steam sanders are also working to counteract any tendency to slip that may might occur for the rails can be greasy in the station. The first coach is also ex L.M.S. "Porthole" stock. The platform extension has been removed and not every train was scheduled to stop. What passengers there were were shepherded to the guard's coach who would also collect the tickets from alighting passengers. Once the train had resumed its journey he would deal with passengers who boarded at the station and excess book them to Glyndyfrdwy where they would re-book to their destination. *Photo: E.N.Kneale.*

BERWYN TO DEESIDE LOOP

The line continues to climb at 1 in 80 beyond Berwyn station and runs high above the Dee before levelling out. A rocky promontory forces the line to tunnel through Berwyn mountain which was one of the major obstacles for the construction company. The tunnel is unlined, after the initial brick facing at both ends, and headroom clearance is limited. Its length is 689 yards, and the track curves throughout. The gradient falls away and at 8 miles 62 chains from Llangollen Line Junction reaches Deeside Loop, slightly above the river level.

62. Berwyn. 10th September 1956. Pannier tank No.5416, formerly of Southall (81C) shed, built in 1931 and fitted with push-pull control apparatus leaves Berwyn with the 1/05pm Wrexham to Bala " train. The Working Time Table specifies the working as a Class B Rail Motor. The normal practice was to use two driving trailers and auto-fitted locomotives which were power classification 1P. At peak holiday times this working was strengthened using spare coaching stock from the district and a more powerful locomotive. The unit worked back to Wrexham with the 3/25pm from Bala and carried the school children from Bala County School to the intermediate halts and Corwen. Notice the old road signs on the bridge complete with the red triangle, and the diamond shaped 'weight restriction' notice for road users. Until the extension to Deeside Halt was opened in April 1990, the Llangollen Railway utilized a run round loop situated just beyond the bridge.

Photo: Norman Jones.

DEESIDE LOOP

This is a single line crossing loop provided solely to break up the long section from Llangollen Goods Line Junction to Glyndyfrdwy. It was provided with a facility which enabled the box to be switched out from the long section, a feature incorporated into the single line Train Staff equipment. The loop, which was on the Up side, could accommodate a train of 45 standard wagons. There was a wooden signal box with an 18 lever frame [5 levers spare] on the Down side. The box was usually switched in during the day and worked by one signalman who was included with the Glyndyfrdwy staff, the operation coming under the control of that stations Station Master. Access to the box was difficult, and a footpath provided the only route from the A5. No platforms were provided. One train a week was scheduled to cross with another in the summer period of 1956, the 12/30pm SO Birkenhead to Barmouth with the 11.10am Pwllheli to Birmingham Snow Hill at 2/28pm.

63. Berwyn. 31st May 1963. The author never traversed Berwyn Tunnel on the footplate of a B.R. Standard Class 4MT but it was known that the crew of No.75021, seen in this photograph would be approaching the portal cautiously. On the more open footplate of a Manor or 63XX class 2-6-0 one was very conscious of the restricted clearance referred to in the text, "Cork in a bottle" being a term several drivers used. The possibility of a "blow back" was always to be guarded against. The regulator would be eased, the blower turned on and the occupants of the footplate would edge judiciously towards the cab sides and away from the firehole door. Due to the curvature of the tunnel one was in Stygian gloom except from the glow from the firebox and the gauge glass lamp. Moreover the crew were very conscious of the heat generated in the confined space and the sulphrous fumes beating down from the tunnel walls and roof into the cab. Very little imagination was necessary to visualise the well documented plight of nineteenth century locomen, marooned with overloaded trains or engine failure in the middle of some tunnel. The eventual circle of light at the exit of Berwyn tunnel was always very welcome.

Photo: Peter E.Baughan.

64. Deeside Loop. c.1964.   *Photo: H.Leadbetter.*

DEESIDE LOOP

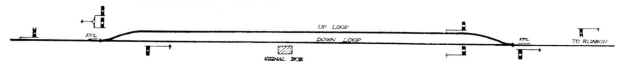

No.**7824** 'Iford Manor' and 43xx No.**7310** are seen approaching Glydyfrydwy with the Festiniog Railway Society special on 22nd April 1961. Readers with a present day interest in the preserved Llangollen Railway will find this view somewhat familiar!

D.J. Lowe Archive

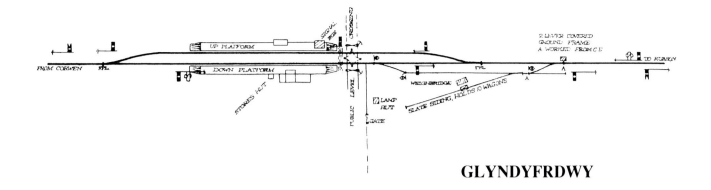

GLYNDYFRDWY

DEESIDE LOOP TO GLYNDYFRDWY

The track is level at Deeside but shortly after rises at 1 in 156 before falling at 1 in 80 as Glyndyfrdwy is approached. Generally the line follows the course of the river up the valley whilst the main A5 road climbs over the hill, taking a shorter route. Road, rail and river converge at different levels but taking roughly parallel routes, with the rail route running into Glyndyfrdwy station, eleven miles from Ruabon station.

GLYNDYFRDWY

The station was located on the edge of and slightly below the village, and was a crossing and token exchange station, connecting with Llangollen Goods Line Junction toward Ruabon when Deeside Loop was switched out, and with Carrog or Corwen East in the Barmouth direction. The main buildings were on the Down side, built of brick and comprising a Booking Office, General Waiting Room, Ladies Waiting Room, two lavatories and a corrugated sheet lamp hut. A Station Masters house was incorporated into the structure. On the Up platform, facilities were limited to a general Waiting Room and lavatories. A signal cabin, containing 24 levers, was located on the Up platform and which also controlled the level crossing at the Ruabon end. On the Llangollen side of the level crossing on the Down side was a small yard of two sidings, access to which was by a small two lever ground frame locked by a key on the Electric Train Staff. No.1. siding could hold 13 wagons and had a load

gauge over it. No 2 siding held 9 wagons and had a truck weighbridge. The Moelferna Slate Quarries provided much of the traffic from the station. The goods yard also contained a cart weighbridge and there was a small warehouse and a crane with a lifting capacity of three tons. In 1925 there were five staff employed, a Class 5 Station Master, three signalmen, of which one was employed at Deeside Loop, and a porter signalman.

Principal traffic from the station in 1924 was Goods, which was about double the passenger traffic receipts.

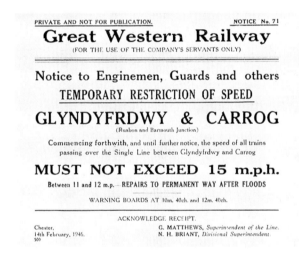

65. **Glyndyfrdwy.** Taken from the Up platform looking towards Llangollen and Ruabon, this view shows the station as it usually looked during the day between trains. The level crossing gates are across the line. the signals are at danger and there is little signs of life, although there would be a signalman on duty and station staff inside the main building on the Down platform. Note the corrugated iron shed used for storage of goods, and a similar building beyond the level crossing, painted cream which was used as a warehouse. Three benches are provided, one on the Up platform. Note the steps in front of the platform gas lamp post. The main station building is constructed of stone, whilst the shelter on the Up platform is constructed of Ruabon red brick, as is the base of the signal cabin.

Photo: Speed Publications.

66. Glyndyfrdwy. 31st May 1963. Because Deeside Loop Signal Box was switched out, the 7.17am from Ruabon to Barmouth was booked to cross the 7.12am Bala to Ruabon train at Glyndyfrdwy. The latter, standing in the Up loop, awaits the arrival of No.**75021**, whose fireman looks ahead for the signalman. Note the signal box on the Up platform. There is quite a queue of road traffic at the level crossing, a double deck lorry conveying sheep to market being prominent, reminds us of trade that was once an important constituent of freight loadings on the branch. The Down slate sidings were behind and to the left of the train. *Photo: Peter E. Baughan.*

67. Glyndyfrdwy. The main station building on the Down side stands beyond the level crossing gates, opposite the signal box and shelter containing a General Waiting Room and two lavatories. As with most of the stations on the line, there was little sign of development and there is a timeless unhurried atmosphere about the platform. The gas lamps are a prominent feature and the absence of passengers is not unusual. There was some seasonal traffic, but by and large, the freight business provided most of the income for the station over the years.

Photo: Speed Publications.

68. Glyndyfrdwy. 1964. Looking east. The buildings on the Up side were typical of the smaller stations along the route, Acrefair setting the pattern. The hipped roofed, Ruabon red brick built signal box adjacent to the level crossing was one of a batch installed c.1898, and replacing a primitive version dating from 1877. The mock Tudor influence is again apparent in the pattern of tall chimneys, whilst glazed bricks are a recurring feature and form a decorative design around the doorway of the Gentlemen's lavatory. The awning does not present any unusual features, but the duo of platform seats, the joint work of Swindon Foundry and the Carriage Shops, would, according to current press reports on "Railwayana", be valuable today. A handsome lantern, designed to shelter a long-burning oil lamp is fitted to either a No.1. or No.2. type post. According to the date of installation, the Stores Department, during a re-organisation, deliberately transposed the reference numbers. *Photo:G.H.Platt.*

Ex GWR 0-6-0PT No.**9752** brings a two coach Bala to Ruabon local passenger train into Glyndyfrdwy, early 1960's. Starting out from Bala at 5.35pm and stopping at all stations, including Corwen at 6.00pm, arrival here at Glyndyfrdwy indicated a departure at 6.12pm. Llangollen would be reached by 6.30pm with the connection with the main line at Ruabon arriving at 6.49pm.

D. J. Lowe Archive

Ex GWR 53XX mogul 2-6-0 No.**5399** draws into Glyndyfrdwy with a Ruabon to Barmouth express passenger working. The engine was shedded at Croes Newydd and was a 'regular' loco seen on the line at the time of this 1960 view.

D. J. Lowe Archive

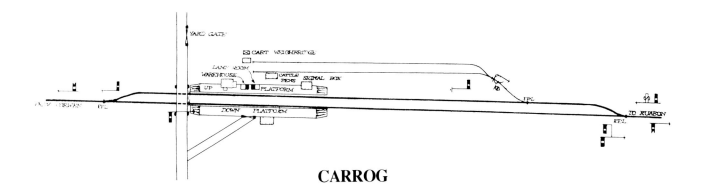

CARROG

GLYNDYFRDWY TO CARROG

The line continued to rise, following the course of the River Dee through the valley, with the hills on either side maintaining a gentle climb, although the gradients were less severe now at 1 in 737, stiffening slightly to 1 in 352 for the next two miles. There are a few occupation crossings in the two miles but nothing of any note. The line runs into Carrog station, thirteen miles from Ruabon and still keeping the river close company.

CARROG

Carrog is provided with a crossing loop and token exchange equipment, but rarely used for that purpose. The layout consisted of a loop with the entry road in line with the main line. A two arm bracket signal facing Barmouth bound trains controlled access to the small yard on the Up side which had two sidings that could house a total of forty five wagons. The shorter siding was provided with a horse landing and cattle pens, a facility that provided most of the freight traffic although general goods as well as lime, coal and timber were handled regularly. A load gauge was provided over the no.1. siding. A small goods warehouse was situated on the Up platform and the yard contained a cart weighbridge. Only Down direction freight trains called to pick up or set down in the yard.

The main buildings were on the Up side, and provided a Booking Office, General Waiting Room, Ladies Waiting Room with its own lavatory, gentlemens toilets and a lamp room. A house for the Station Master was integral with the structure which was built of stone. Also on the Up platform was a signal cabin which housed a frame of twenty levers and controlled all points and signals. The Down platform contained a General Waiting Room and a urinal. The B5437 road passed over the tracks by a stone overbridge from the A5 to Carrog village, some half a mile from the station. Possibly because of the distance, rail traffic from Carrog was less than at Glyndyfrdwy, although the village itself was larger. Staff at the station comprised a Station Master, class 5 and two porter signalmen. Token Equipment was provided and the sections were to Glyndyfrdwy in the east and Corwen East box in the Barmouth direction, although Carrog signal box could be switched out, in which case the circuit was from Glyndyfrdwy to Corwen East.

69, Carrog. c.1955. Taken from the road overbridge at the west end of the station and looking towards Ruabon, this view shows the compact layout of the station. The main buildings were on the Up platform as was the signal cabin, which housed a 19 lever frame. The Down platform shelter was brick built, in contrast to the stone structure for the main building. The station had a well kept appearance and the station staff took a pride in ensuring that the shrubs were kept neat and tidy. The goods yard sidings are empty but freight traffic from the station was mainly livestock and varied according to the season. The line curves away towards Glyndyfrdwy and the two arm bracket signal has the Down direction right hand arm lowered which indicated that the train signalled would proceed to the Up loop line or into the goods yard.
Photo: Speed Publications.

70. Carrog. c.1955. Track renewal and maintenance on the single line involved total line occupation, and as such were confined to night time and Sundays. Careful planning was necessary, including the need to ensure that the locomotive was suitably placed to enable relief crews to change over during the day. It was also necessary to ensure that locomotives had adequate water supply to last the shift. In this view, the Permanent Way department were unloading sleepers and loading spent ballast between Glyndyfrdwy and Carrog. 0-6-0 Pannier tank engine No.**8734** stands at the head of a raft of wagons which have been divided for working purposes. At changeover time, the train would work filled wagons to Carrog, which they would leave in the siding. The relieving set worked a light engine from Bala to Carrog where they exchanged footplates with the first set who returned L.E. to Bala. The opportunity was taken to top up the tank before returning to the site.   *Photo: A.Donaldson.*

71. Carrog. An Edwardian air to this fine period view of Carrog, with the Class 5 Stationmaster wearing across his waistcoat a heavy chain to one end of which will be attached his pocket watch and to the other a balancing medallion. Behind him, the magnificent station-house, although the internal appointments in those days would probably have been less grand than the exterior. However, just after World War I, the rental would only be 3/9d per week, including rates. The porter-signalman, in the fashion of the day carries his watch on a single chain in the left hand upper pocket of his sleeved waistcoat. The nameboard typified G.W.R. practise, the front of the board being painted black, the cast-iron letters, frame, and moulding white. The back of the board and the posts - which were of the standard pattern previously described - were a Stores issue standard tint, all as prescribed by Swindon. Worthy of note is the cast-iron post supporting the fine oil lamp, the post unusual in being fluted throughout its length. Note the filler and regulator can be seen inside the lamp housing.   *Photo: G.Biddle collection.*

72. Carrog. c.1955. An August idyll, the platform busy, with ladies disporting themselves in bright summer dresses. Observe the corrugated-iron Goods Warehouse and Lamp Room, the family group on the platform seat, and the figure of a young lady jauntily sitting on the wall, probably a holidaying visitor, staying in the splendidly clerestoried Camping Coach in the siding. The four-wheeled van standing near to the cattle-pens looks remarkably like one of Pooley's travelling tool-vans, always despatched in advance of the fitters making their scheduled visit, so it is assumed that the weighbridge in the yard is due for overhaul. Completing this encapsulation of a typical scene on this much loved line is one of Mr.C.B.Collett's 2-6-0's, which drifts beneath the public road bridge with a Class A Barmouth to Chester train.
                            Photo: Speed Publications.

CARROG TO CORWEN

The line resumed a single track beyond the road overbridge and varied in gradient rising and generally following the contour of the valley but never straying very far from the river. After just under one mile, Carrog Slate Siding, located on the Down side of the line was reached. This was a private siding but maintained by the G.W.R. at the Quarry Companys expense. Access to the siding, which was worked by a ground frame was by a key on the electric train staff which unlocked the frame. Slate was carried to the siding by an incline tramway. The siding came under the supervision of the Carrog Station Master. The A5 road converged on the railway and river as the valley closed in and the three kept company with each other for about half a mile before the valley widened slightly. The area was prone to flooding and when the Dee burst its banks, there was a tendency for the line to be flooded at this point with some erosion of the trackbed, which ensured that the District Civil Engineer kept a watchful eye on the river levels. Contingency plans were constantly under review. The GWR. was mindful of this situation

occurring in this and other parts of North and Mid Wales, and produced a pamphlet [Notice N.W.500] entitled "Diversion of Trains to Alternative Routes in cases of Emergency" which was revised periodically and which outlined the procedure to be adopted.

BONWM

In the 1920s, the G.W.R. in an attempt to increase traffic on the line opened a small halt called Bonwm about half way between Carrog and Corwen, the name being taken from a small hamlet close by. The platform was a very basic affair on the Down side, just over seventy feet in length, with a wooden shelter, nameboard and an electric lamp, which the guard of convenient trains were required to switch on and off. Passenger access to the platform was by a footpath from the A5. Much skill was required on the part of drivers to stop with the Guard's coach at the platform. Not every train stopped at the halt, some being shown as 'conditional', but there must have been sufficient traffic to justify its retention. The guard was initially responsible for booking passengers from the halt to either Carrog or Corwen, then informing the booking clerk there of the details of passengers uplifted, who were then re-booked on. Passengers being set down at Bonwm had their tickets collected by the guard. There were no facilities for parcels or freight traffic, these being dealt with by Corwen. The halt remained operational until the premature closure of the line in 1964.

73. Bonwm. 10th June 1956. 43XX Class 2-6-0 No.**7313**, of Croes Newydd (84J) has just left Carrog, (the Up home signal can be seen in the exact centre of the photograph in the "V" between the trees), and, swinging round beside the River Dee and the slopes of Llantysilio Mountain, runs parallel to the Holyhead road on the approach to Bonwm Halt. There is a feather of steam from the cylinder cocks, and the fireman was rather anxiously looking down over the cab-side at the injector overflow pipe.
Photo: Norman Jones.

74. Bonwm. 31st May 1963. The entry for Bonwm Halt appeared in the Working Time Tables as: Mileage from Llangollen Line Junction 14m 12³/₄ch, Gradient 1 in 792R Against train 2J53 at 8Z05am. Reference to the footnotes provided the following information. "**Z** calls at Bonwm Halt, Saturdays and School Holidays excepted (not advertised) to pick up passengers only. Perhaps the driver of No.**75021** is looking out for his regular passengers as he carefully brings his train up to the short platform. Right until the end, there was a great spirit of service amongst all staff and a public appreciation of their efforts, indeed, many of them were on first name terms.
Photo: Peter E.Baughan.

An unidentified 0-6-0PT on a short Goods working for Ruabon is seen leaving Corwen, in May 1961. The loco is likely to have originated from Bala where the depot will have provided the Pannier from one of its allocation of 57's at the time. The double bolster wagon is carrying lengths of rail, which suggests the PW Department have been busy somewhere down the line.

D. J. Lowe Archive

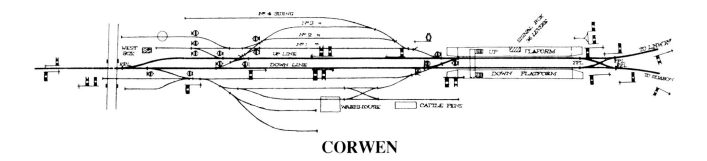

CORWEN

CORWEN

Corwen was a busy market town serving a population of about four thousand and drawing business from a wide geographical area. Agriculture was the main source of employment when the line was open and which also provided much of the revenue for the railways. It was the largest intermediate station on the line and sixteen miles from Ruabon. It was also the terminus for the LNWR/LMS branch from Ruthin and Denbigh which crossed the Dee over a lattice girder multi-span bridge before making an end on connection with the G.W.R. at the Ruabon end of the station. The station overall was in excess of half a mile in length, and controlled by two signal boxes. Track between the East and West boxes was double and worked under Double Line Absolute Block Regulations.

The main buildings, part of which survive, were brick built and located on the Down platform and comprised a Booking Hall, Booking Office, Parcels Office, Station Masters Office, District Inspectors Office, Guards Room, General Waiting Room, Ladies Waiting Room, Refreshment Rooms, various stores Rooms and two lavatories. There was also a road motor garage built of corrugated iron sheet, adjoining. The Up side platform contained a General Waiting Room, Ladies Waiting Room and two lavatories. The East Signal Cabin was located on the Up platform and was built of red brick. Passenger access between the platform was by a standard GWR design footbridge which was totally enclosed until the late 1950s when the corrugated sheet cover and windows were removed. Some of the station staff were employed jointly with the LMS who also had certain booking rights. The Station Staff consisted a Station Master - Class 2, Goods Clerk, 2 General Clerks, Junior Clerk, 2 Shunters, 4 Signalmen, Porter Signalman, Checker, Goods Porter, Parcels Porter, 1 Porter grade 1, 3 Porters grade 2, and a Junior Numbertaker, all on the joint account. In addition, the GWR employed a District Inspector, 3 Goods Guards and 1 Signalman. Goods traffic receipts for 1924 were double the passenger figures with Parcels traffic contributing significantly and the total receipts for the year amounted to £16,750. Wages amounted to £5612 but it is not certain whether this included the Locomotive Department staff.

Corwen East signal box contained a frame with 34 levers. It had Electric Train Staff connection with Gwyddelwern on the L.M.S. Vale of Clwyd line and was connected with the Denbigh District telephone circuit. It had an Electric Train Staff connection with Carrog, when that station was switched into the circuit, and Key Token equipment with Glyndyfrdwy when Carrog was switched out.

The Goods Yard was located at the Barmouth end of the station, and straddled the running lines. On the Up side, the siding accommodation consisted of five sidings, with a storage capacity of one hundred wagons, of which the Cattle Pen siding accounted for twenty. Also on the Up side were two sidings known as the West End. No 1 siding, which housed 28 wagons was the shunting spur whilst No.2. siding could store 10 wagons. On the Down side were five sidings with a wagon capacity of 115 wagons. The warehouse which could house four wagons was on the Down side and adjoining the A5 road. The building itself contained two cranes each with a lifting capacity of 30cwts. The warehouse siding had a load gauge installed. A weighbridge was provided in the mileage yard and there was a yard crane with a lifting capacity of eight tons.

Corwen West box was located on the Up side of the running lines, was smaller in size than East box and housed a 24

75. Corwen. c.1932. Corwen, between the wars, looking east towards Ruabon. The two-doll bracket signal on its wooden post, and the cross-overs with their facing point locks, mark to the left of the picture, the divergence from the main line of what was the the L.M.S. (former L.N.W.R.) Ruthin-Denbigh branch. Observe the foliate effect the painter has applied to the standard of the water column and the reflector fitted to direct the light from the gas lamp. The Setting Down Post, at the foot of the opposite ramp, is not fitted with the ropework safety net, this being a feature of later days. *Photo: G.H.Platt.*

lever frame. It controlled entry to the west end of the Goods sidings and marked the resumption of the single track main line. This was worked to Llandrillo by Electric Train Staff.

The Locomotive Department was located on the Up side, at the Ruabon end of the site with the building behind the West End Signal Box. This contained a single pit road. A 55ft. turntable was provided. Alongside the Turntable road was a pillar tank that supplied columns at the Ruabon end of the Up platform, the Barmouth end of the Down platform and one outside the Locomotive shed. Until 1927 there were seven sets of GWR men based here. Their work extended to Wrexham, Blaenau Ffestiniog and Barmouth Junction, although most of it was between Bala and Ruabon. When the GWR took the decision to close the shed in 1927 it is believed but not confirmed that most of the work

and the men were transferred to Bala, with only three men transferring to Croes Newydd or beyond. The closure of the shed had implications for the LMS, who had three sets of men outstationed here. The LMS were unwilling to take over the shed and transferred its men to Denbigh. However the shed road and turntable remained and in use until the mid 1950s although the building was removed some two decades earlier.

The Traffic Department retained its Goods Guards for some time after the removal of the Locomotive Departments, although the Passenger Guards were relocated before 1930. It is believed but not confirmed that four GWR Passenger Guards and Two LMS Guards were affected. It is possible that some men accepted demotion to the status of Porter Guard rather than move away. Details of their work have not yet surfaced.

76. Corwen. 31st May 1963. The 8.00am arrival of No.**75021** with the Ruabon to Barmouth train finds the signalman from Corwen East Box waiting in the 'six foot' to collect the token, two minutes being allowed for station duties. Of note is the rather complicated rodding and connections beneath the platform to the signal box. Over the rods, the wooden stepping is provided for the convenience of the signalmen. Other interesting features are the rather unsightly modification to the lamp post, capped with telephone insulators, whilst adjacent, there is an antiquated single-wheeled flat bed barrow. Although the footbridge has lost its roof the supporting brackets still remain at the foot of the staircase. The General and Ladies Waiting Rooms and Lavatories are of a similar design to those found on smaller stations.
Photo: Peter E.Baughan.

77. Corwen. September 1963. The freight working from Denbigh, having completed its duties in the Down siding, draws alongside the Up platform, the fireman going to the signalman to collect the 'Webb-Thompson' Staff giving clearance for a 1/30pm departure to the next crossing point at Gwyddelwern en-route to Ruthin. We see the unusual ridge and furrow formation of the awning on the Up side, the rear portions glazed, the front comprising corrugated-iron sheeting. The curved and straight edges of the pediments, and the triangular lining is effective as is the pattern drilled beneath the eaves in the boarded ends. An interesting platform survivor is a wicker G.P.O. two-wheeled trolley. The train engine, 2MT 2-6-0 No.**46509** is one of Mr Ivatt's taper boiler design based on L.M.S. practice and introduced from 1946.
Photo: R.E.G.Read.
G.Biddle collection.

78. Corwen. 31st January 1953. A sombre scene at Corwen as No.**40671**, of Rhyl (6K) Shed but outstationed at Denbigh, halts beneath a footbridge in deplorable condition. Small wonder that later the roof would be removed as being beyond economical repair. The Denbigh, Ruthin & Corwen Railway opened from Ruthin to a temporary station at Corwen in September 1864, and to the "joint" station twelve months later. Absorbed by the L.& N.W.R. Co. in 1879, the branch became part of the L.M.S. system at the grouping. Traffic diminished after the Second World War and the passenger service was discontinued on 2nd. February 1953. This photograph shows the 12/05pm train on the last day of public service. A seemingly run down No.40671 has **BRITISH RAIL-WAYS** emblazoned on the tender.

Photo: W.A.Camwell.

79. Corwen. 31st May 1963. Most Down trains took water at Corwen, and No.**75021** was no exception, but with only two minutes stop-over time booked, the fireman had to work quickly, pushing coal down on to the tender flap-plate whilst the tender water-tank was being topped up. The open saloon, with its yellow stripe and shining windows mirrors buildings in the station yard, probably the result of a recent visit for cleaning. The driver is hidden from view behind the water column, waiting to turn the flow off. Notice the chimney for the brazier which was used to heat the water column in times of frost, with its chimney 'pot'. This pattern could frequently be seen on the roof of signal boxes. The platform lamp appears to be a hybrid design also. *Photo: Peter E.Baughan.*

80. Corwen. c.1960. A definitive view of the extensive yard and sidings at Corwen, seen in this photograph taken from the footbridge and facing towards the West End signal box, main road overbridge and Bala Junction. Regretfully by this time traffic was dwindling at Corwen where, as at other rail-freight depots, customers who were lost to road haulage during the 1955 loco-mens strike rarely returned. Most of the features shown on the track plan can readily be identified in this scene. Note the goods yard signal with the white ring over the arm, the scissors crossover in front of the goods shed and the empty cattle pens which once were hosts to a regular and thriving element of freight traffic. In the distance can be seen the water tank which stood on the former engine shed road. *Photo: Speed Publications.*

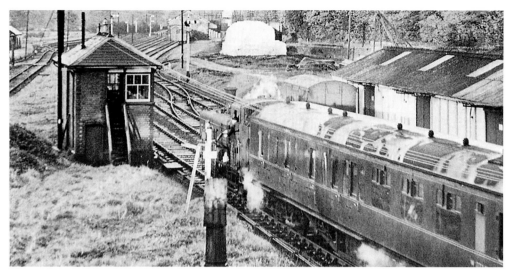

81. Corwen. 5th October 1963, 57xx Class pannier tank No.**4683** with three coaches working the 5/40pm from Bala to Wrexham approaches Corwen West signal box and slows to the regulation 10 mph as the fireman slips the hoop of the token carrier over the receiving arm outside the box, before entering the double line section to the station. The yard is almost deserted, with a short rake of vans standing in front of the Goods Shed in the yard on the Down side whilst another van stands in front of the private store opposite the box. This duty was once an auto train working but latterly was worked with ordinary coaching stock. The locomotive turn was a Bala working, and at Wrexham the crew would go on Croes Newydd shed, where they would prepare a fresh engine and rejoin the stock in the station, returning to Bala at 9/28pm. *Photo: M.Mensing.*

82. Corwen. 19th May 1961. The exit 'road' from the Warehouse and adjoining road at Corwen with the station in view over the cab roof of 0-6-0 3F No.**43610**, Driver Bill Jones and Fireman Emrys Ingleby on the footplate and about to work a return freight to Ruthin and Denbigh. On the left, a rake of cattle trucks. Livestock trains ran under any of Class C, D, or E identities under the provisions of B.R. Rule No.171 (Rule Book issue dated 1st January 1950 and subsequent amendments). Such traffic had been regulated for many years. "Cattle - shunting of ..... Rule 256A" featured in the "GREAT WESTERN AND MIDLAND JOINT RAILWAYS. Rules and Regulations. FOR THE GUIDANCE of the OFFICERS and MEN ...... On their Joint Railways, and at their Joint Stations". dated July 1885. Notice also the somewhat spartan cab layout, with little regard for the comfort of footplate crew. *Photo: Norman Jones.*

83. Corwen. April 1961. Corwen: West End. The 8.10am freight from Denbigh has drawn its train through station limits and now No.**43618** propels the four coal empties, exchanged for four loaded wagons left at Eyarth along the shunting neck and into the Down sidings, to shunt the yard, as required, and make up the rake for its return trip. That done the train will draw forward onto the outlet road, stopping beside the goods warehouse where, in the period before departure time the crew will foregather in the guard's van for lunch. Hosted for some years by a Denbigh guard, the late Arthur Davies, these were happy occasions where one experienced an atmosphere unique to an industry where generations of the same families served the railway, and whose communities were ruthlessly abandoned in the name of modernisation. *Photo: Norman Jones.*

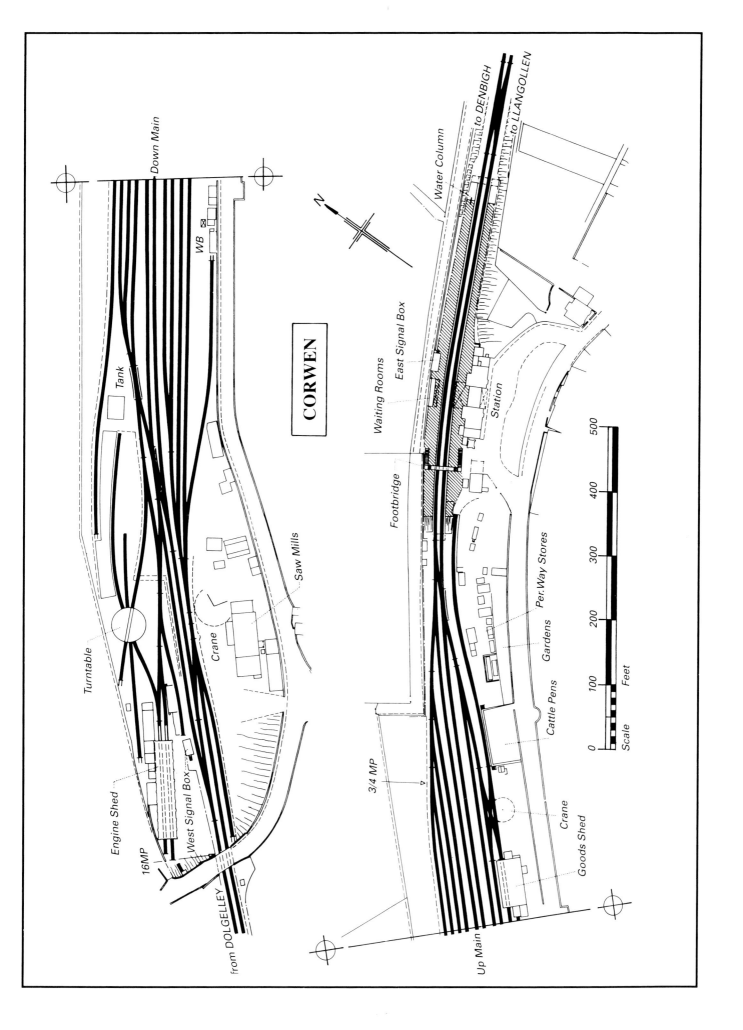

CORWEN

Down Main

WB

Tank

Turntable

Engine Shed

16MP

West Signal Box

from DOLGELLEY

Crane

Saw Mills

N

Waiting Rooms

East Signal Box

Footbridge

Water Column

to DENBIGH

to LLANGOLLEN

Station

Per.Way Stores

Gardens

Cattle Pens

3/4 MP

Up Main

Crane

Goods Shed

0   100   200   300   400   500

Scale   Feet

Corwen, 9th May 1949. British Railways have quickly applied their mark – in the form of a smokebox number plate – but otherwise this is a view of an LMS train in a Great Western station. LMS built Compound 4-4-0 Class 4P No 40933 (6A – Chester) awaits departure time with the 2.25 pm train to Chester via Denbigh and Mold, a distance of 48 miles taking in nineteen intermediate stations for the 140 minute journey. The London Midland Region timetable did not acknowledge the fact that Corwen also served trains on the Ruabon to Barmouth line, probably because a journey to or from Chester could be up to one hour quicker and fifteen miles shorter. The appearance of a Compound on this service was somewhat unusual as it was normally diagrammed for a class 2P 4-4-0. The locomotive seen here was one of a batch of ten built at the Vulcan Foundry in 1927. After only three decades of service it was withdrawn in 1957 following brief spells at Monument Lane (Birmingham) and Normanton.

Photo: E.S. Russell.

84. Corwen. 19th May 1961. Holyhead Road overbridge and Corwen West Signal Box, at about 11.30am, ex Midland Railway Class 3F 0-6-0 No.43698, in the charge of Driver Bill Jones and Fireman Emrys Ingleby of Denbigh shed, having brought the daily Class K freight from Denbigh and come down through the Vale of Clwyd, making calls at Ruthin, Eyarth, Nantclwyd, Derwen and Gwyddelwern (the staff exchange point), has propelled into the yard and will run round its train. General shunting is in progress and an end-tipping wagon containing rubble is being disposed of. Shunting hooks and poles were very personalised, each having its own "feel", and Guard Arthur Davies and the Yard Foreman having got theirs mixed, lose no time in effecting an exchange. This duty was one of the last four turns which remained at Denbigh, only two drivers remaining there, which was an outstation of Rhyl (6K) shed. *Photo: Norman Jones.*

85. Corwen. April 1961. An eastward facing view of Corwen West End and signal box, taken from the A5 road overbridge. To the right are the rail served storage sheds, and to the left the site of the former locomotive shed, the 55 foot turntable still in position and operative, whilst the massive water tank stands four-square. Associated with the tower was an electrical water-pumping plant with a linked warning bell installed in the signal box which would ring in the event of failure. In this event the West signalman was instructed to "proceed to the engine house" and carry out a complicated "failure and restart" routine. Furthermore a "pump cut-off switch" was installed in the box and was operated whenever the signalman opened or closed Corwen West Signal Box. Observe the setting down post, 21 yards on the Bala side of the box. A picking up post was not required, the section to Corwen West being double-track. *Photo: Norman Jones.*

86.Corwen. c.1963. Another aspect of B.R. Standard Class 4MT 4-6-0 No.75021, seen on an overcast day with the River Dee in spate, approaching Corwen West with an Up five coach Class B passenger train. Behind the leading brake-composite coach can be observed the Home Signal, lever No.24, in the 25 lever West box frame. The Down shunting neck on the left ended at a timber stop-block, observe that the bull-head rail is laid in chairs secured to concrete blocks held to gauge by tie rods, with twin rods at rail joints, where each length ended with a tie bar. On the extreme right of the picture can be seen the Down direction token picking up post, 90 yards from Corwen West signal box with the lamp in place to illuminate the token at night *Photo: Derek Cross.*

No.**7827** 'Lydham Manor' and 2-6-2T No.**4555** are seen leaving Corwen bound for the coast, with the TRPS Special on 26th September 1964. It is the ultimate aim of the Llangollen Railway to reach Corwen, from Llangollen, but it is highly unlikely we will ever see a train departure, as in this view, of one setting out westwards from here again for the 'coast'.

D. J. Lowe Archive

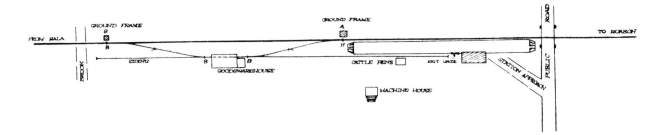

CORWEN TO CYNWYD

On leaving Corwen station the line passed between the sidings on either side of the running lines and almost to the road bridge under the A5 road. The single line resumed at Corwen West Signal Box where the Electric Train Staff was collected for the section between Corwen West and Llandrillo, four and a half miles distant. The line again followed the course of the Dee for much of the way and the initial section was on a rising gradient of 1 in 200. The proximity to the river ultimately caused the closure of the line albeit in the period after initial closure in 1964 and the resumption of trains whilst the replacement bus service was introduced.

Within half a mile of leaving Corwen a minor road was crossed at Llangar Church. The crossing was provided with block indicators which were located in the cottage and was attended by the wife of a lengthman who received the princely sum of 4/- for her duties in 1927. Ironically she was deducted 2/6d [12.5p] of this for rent for the cottage. Despite its proximity to Corwen, the crossing came under the supervision of the Cynwyd Station Master.

CYNWYD

The station, which was not a Block Post, consisted of a single platform and a siding, which could house 28 wagons, both on on the Down side of the line. The siding passed through a Goods Warehouse which was 36ft. in length. A load gauge was provided over the siding, and there was a cart weighbridge in the yard. Cattle pens were located behind the passenger platform. The two ground frames, East and West, at each end of the siding connections were locked by the key on the Electric Train Staff. The station buildings were constructed of brick and comprised a Booking Office, General Waiting Room, Ladies Waiting Room and two lavatories. A house was acquired for the Station master in 1924 but this was located away from the station in the village.

The station staff was made up of a Station Master [Class 5], a gatewoman, and a porter, who also attended to the lamps at Llandderfel, Llandrillo and Corwen. In 1924, receipts from Goods traffic, which was of a general nature including a regular flow of cattle traffic exceeded Passenger and Parcels traffic. There had been some competition from Crosville in the summer of 1925 but insufficient to justify retention of the service into the winter.

87. Cynwyd. July 1963. Although Cynwyd did not officially close for goods traffic until 4th May 1964, the outer wall of the warehouse, and part of the roof have been demolished. Although the wall-footings remain, the former warehouse 'through' line is flanked by them together with the remains of the goods loading bay. However, there has been a road-haulage 'invasion' in the form of articulated timber carrying drags in the yard yet, as late as 1960, much of this traffic was rail-borne, and special instructions appeared in the Appendix to the Working Time Tables to ensure the safety of "TRAINS ON LINE" when loading of long timber was in progress. *Photo: R.E.G.Read. G.Biddle Collection.*

88. Cynwyd. c.1960. This view of Cynwyd, from the public road overbridge, 17m 66ch from Llangollen Line Junction typifies the basic G.W.R. rural station, and has much of interest. The station buildings are a slightly enlarged version of the standard design, and a notable feature is the inlaid patterns of glazed facing bricks around the groins and arches of lavatory doors and windows, the latter fitted with louvres. Economically the platform was only flagged in front of the Booking Office and Waiting Rooms. Left of centre we observe the goods warehouse and right, beyond the broad meadow the waters of the burgeoning Afon Dyfrdwy. Notice the battered firebuckets which would never have been tolerated prior to 1955, and the signs of neglect. The goods shed is complete in this view, although the windows of the goods office have been boarded up.

Photo: Speed Publications.

89. Cynwyd. 1964. In the final summer of the line's operation, this view was taken from a Barmouth bound train looking back towards Corwen, and shows the road overbridge from where the two previous photographs were taken. The small canopy affords little protection to the traveller, but is clean and fresh as if it had been painted recently. The nameboard is still typical G.W.R. design with screw on letters. One name-board post is out of alignment. Two lamps flank the building which would have provided scant illumination during hours of darkness. Notice the ornate chimney stacks, which must have provided a good draught to the fires in the waiting room and the offices.

Photo: G.H.Platt.

90. Cynwyd. 7th October 1960 Mist shrouded the valley at 10.20am when leaving Cynwyd on the footplate of 2-6-0 No.**6357**. The siding traversed the 36ft long goods warehouse, built of coursed masonry, the red and white chequered plate on the end wall warning traincrews of the restricted clearance. Concerning the ground frames (see text) the west frame is to the right of the connection, Points 1B and 1A, and in the four-foot is the ramp protecting the rodding. The relevant Facing Point Lock was No.2., No.1. being at the east end. *Photo: Norman Jones.*

G.W.R.

Llandrillo

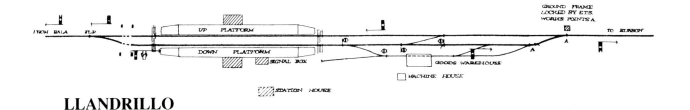

LLANDRILLO

CYNWYD TO LLANDRILLO

The line to Llandrillo, a little over two and a half miles away, was practically level and maintained its course close to the river up the valley. Periodically, timber was loaded at the lineside, this being done on Sundays, when the section of line between Corwen and Llandrillo was occupied for several hours at a time. Specific instructions were set down in the Sectional Appendix to the Working Time Tables whenever this operation took place. The locomotive was always located at the Bala end, and at the commencement of the work, the train was worked to Llandrillo in the normal fashion. The locomotive was then run round the train which was propelled to the loading site. A brake van was located at each end. To effect the change of train crew, the train was worked back to Bala and returned in the same way as the morning turn. At the end of the day the train worked back to Bala in the normal way. There were several different locations where timber was located and these varied according to requirements.

LLANDRILLO

The station was provided with a crossing loop on the Down side, the platform containing the main station buildings which comprised a Booking Office, General Waiting Room, Ladies Waiting Room and 2 lavatories. The Up platform had a General Waiting Room and Urinals. Passengers crossed the line at the foot of the platform ramps. A Signal Cabin was located on the Down platform and housed a frame of twenty four levers, of which six were spare. The goods yard consisted of a loop, which housed 25 wagons, No.1. siding holding 9 wagons and No.2, which could accommodate 29 wagons. A small corrugated iron warehouse was located in the goods yard holding a crane with a lifting capacity of 1 ton. A loading gauge stood over No.1. siding. The Station Masters house was also located in the yard. Originally entrance to the goods yard was controlled by a ground frame at the Ruabon end, which was locked by the key on the train staff, but this was altered and control effected from the signal cabin and the ground frame removed around 1926.

The station staff consisted of a Station Master, class 5, and two class 5 signalmen working alternate shifts. The Cynwyd porter attended to the lamps and some station duties. Goods traffic revenue was about twice the Passenger returns in 1924. Token setting down and picking up posts were provided and located close to the signal box in both directions.

91. Llandrillo. c.1960. Maintaining a generations old tradition, Llandrillo's Station Master makes his morning rounds. The G.W.R. Rule Book dated July 1885 contained a complete section, Pages No.s. 50 to 63 inclusive, covering his duties and responsibilities, and many of the provisions appearing in the British Railways book of "RULES FOR OBSERVANCE BY EMPLOYEES", dated 1st January 1950 were similar. The stone-built goods shed dwarfs the mineral wagon in the siding. As at Carrog, where the railway could spread itself in the Vale of Edeyrion, the Up and Down side Token Exchange Apparatus is conveniently situated near the signal box. *Photo: Speed Publications.*

92. Llandrillo. 31st May 1963. Our Barmouth-bound train, hauled by B.R. Standard Class 4MT 4-6-0 No.**75021** has now entered Llandrillo and, changing sides the photographer features a westwards facing aspect of the Up platform, particularly the General Waiting Room which we note is built with bricks laid in English Bond, capped with a stylish pediment in two orders and topped by an exuberant chimney stack, the general symmetry enhanced by a plain cap. The rusticated masonry and design of the overbridge are admirably suited to their surroundings. Passenger access to the Up platform was down the ramp and across the trolley walk-way, with warning boards for the clients, overlooked by the signalman.

Photo: Peter E. Baughan.

93. Llandrillo. 5th October 1963. British Railways Standard Class 4MT 4-6-0 No.**75026** with a 6C (Croes Newydd) shedplate and fitted with a double chimney pulls away from Llandrillo with the 1/35pm Chester to Barmouth Class B. train. Steam is available in abundance, as the safety valves blow off furiously, and steam still escaping from the drain cocks, shrouding the motion and partially obscuring the driver's vision of the road ahead. The grass and growth on the embankment on either side of the track have been cut back recently and present a tidy appearance to the observer. There is little sign of activity about the station, the staff no doubt have retreated to the shelter of the office. The locomotive and stock will form the last through train of the day from Barmouth to Chester departing at 7/15pm after attaching through coaches from Pwllheli. *Photo: M.Mensing.*

94. Llandrillo. c.1960. A view looking west of a somnolent Llandrillo. The line curved sharply beyond the overbridge and, out of sight, but adjacent to Point No.10, F.P.L. No.9. was located the Up Home signal - No.2. The Down Starter, No.22, carrying on the same post Subsidiary Signal No.21, can just be seen close to the bridge abutment. Surprisingly, the larger block of buildings including the Booking Office on the Down platform were not complemented by an awning. Notice the recesses in the platform brickwork on either side of the track to accommodate the point rodding and signal wires from the adjacent signal box. The rodding and wires to the Up side pass under the rails and between the sleepers. Notice also the walkway in the six foot. *Photo: Speed Publications.*

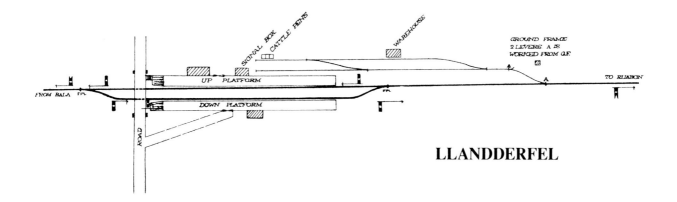

LLANDDERFEL

LLANDRILLO TO LLANDDERFEL

The line resumes its single track formation for the two and a half miles to Llandderfel, which is also the next crossing station and Electric Train Staff exchange point. The line is level for most of the two and a half miles. At one time there was a small platform mid way between the two stations but as this was a private halt, did not feature in the public time tables, and was dispensed with before the outbreak of the second world war. Between the two stations the line passed over the river twice. Cilan bridge had three arches and was located close to Llandrillo, whilst Dolgadfa bridge comprised two arches and was about a mile from Llandderfel.

LLANDDERFEL

The station served four small settlements of which Llandderfel was the largest and closest to the line. There were two platforms and trains could cross here. The Down line formed the loop which extended beyond the platforms and under a road overbridge before resuming single track. The main buildings were on the Up platform, and comprised a Booking Office, General Waiting Room, Ladies Waiting Room, two lavatories, with a separate coalhouse and lamproom. The signal box was also on the Up platform. A small yard was located on the

Up side, on the Corwen side of the loop and controlled by a ground frame locked by a key on the Electric Train Staff. A goods warehouse was located midway along No.2. siding, with a crane of 1 ton capacity. At the end of the siding, which could hold 18 wagons, were cattle pens. No.1. siding could accommodate 31 wagons and a load gauge was located on this line. The Down platform had a small Waiting Room and a urinal. The Up distant signal controlled a treadle which sounded a warning bell. Here too the Cynwyd porter attended to the oil lamps. There were Electric Train Staff setting down and taking up posts provided in both Up and Down directions located on the Bala Junction side of the signal box.

The station staff here comprised a Station Master class 5 and two class 5 signalmen. Passenger receipts for 1924 were double the goods receipts, but parcels traffic was quite important. The goods traffic dealt with comprised mainly of general goods and some timber.

At one time, Sir Henry Robertson lived in Pale Hall, and Queen Victoria visited there in 1889. There was a close association between the Hall and the station with a telephone link between the signal box and the residence.

95. Llandderfel. Taken from the road overbridge at the west end of the station looking towards Ruabon on a miserable day, this view shows the small goods yard and goods warehouse. The signal cabin contained a 14 lever frame which controlled the passing loop points, point-locks and the signals, but not the access to the goods yard which was operated by a small ground frame locked by the key token. The Down platform shelter boasted a small canopy. Intending passengers travelling west were required to purchase their tickets from the booking office on the Up platform then cross over to the Down side by climbing up a flight of wooden steps to the road, crossing over the bridge and down another flight of steps to gain the platform. It was not unknown for the intrepid to wait until no one was looking and use the barrow crossing at the foot of the ramp, under the road overbridge. At the time of taking the photograph, the staff took great pride in their station keeping it tidy and presentable. A small garden is just visible on the Down platform.
Photo: J.H.Moss.

Another view of 57XX 0-6-0PT No.**9752**, this time seen entering Llandderfel station with a two coach Ruabon-Bala passenger train. An early 1960's view. *D. J. Lowe Archive*

96. Llandderfel. c.1949. 0-6-0PT No. **6405** (Push & Pull fitted) propelling a Bala to Wrexham Motor Train stands at Llandderfel Up platform awaiting the key token. The engine number is displayed G.W.R. fashion on the buffer-beam, but there are no smoke-box or shed-code plates. A Chester to Barmouth Class B train draws into the Down side loop. On the Up platform notice the slate hung end gable of the station building, the corner bracketed oil-lamp and the signalman hastening to the Down platform with the hoop of the token-carrier over his shoulder. The fine topiary near the signal box perhaps highlights the pride in which the railway staff took in their stations. When Queen Victoria stayed in nearby Pale Hall, the Robertson family mansion, during her only visit to Wales, she arrived at Llandderfel by Special train on 23rd August 1889. Unfortunately for the local dignitaries, the driver overshot the red carpet and had to reverse the train!
Photo: Speed Publications.

97. Llandderfel. 7th October 1960. Activity on Llandderfel's Down platform, viewed from the footplate of 2-6-0 No.**6357** on the 7.50am Birkenhead to Pwllheli train. Fireman J.A.Jones has just received the Llandderfel to Bala Junction token from signalman Norman Griffiths and verified it with Driver Roy Sharrock. Stationmaster Llew Thomas gives the "right-away" to Llangollen based Guard Arthur Davies, who, flag raised, authorises our departure (although this does not raise from the driver the responsiblity to ensure that he has a clear road ahead). Mr.Thomas, who had also served at Maentwrog Road, had a brother, Griff, Stationmaster at such disparite locations as Festiniog and Moretonhampstead, whilst brother Jack, at Wrexham, was a Croes Newydd driver.
Photo: Norman Jones.

98. Llandderfel. 1964. An east facing aspect - towards Ruabon - of the Up side platform at Llandderfel, seen from a train on the Down loop which will rejoin the main Down/Up line via Point No.8. F.P.L. No.9. The Down Starting signal was on the Bala Junction side of the overbridge (Lever No.3). but there was a repeater (also Lever 3). on the Ruabon side of the bridge. The Down Home signal (Lever No.2) was protected with a fixed distant. Observed beyond the box, the Up Starter (Lever No.12). working in conjunction with Point No.7., F.P.L. No.6. The station has come to look neglected as staff levels fall, the platform coping needs whitewash, the once shapely bushes have become unkempt, but reminiscent of happier days, the handsome casings for long-burning oil lamps still grace the corners of the station. Note also the flight of open tread wooden steps leading to the roadway, which appear to have been purpose built, and the exit via the white wicket gate on to the station yard. *Photo: G.H.Platt.*

This view taken in July 1957, shows No 7827 'Lydham Manor' travelling eastwards with a Barmouth to Chester express arriving at Bala Junction. Passengers to and from Bala (Town) station were ferried to the junction via a shuttle service, which in the 1950's was in the capable hands of 58xx class 0-4-2 tank locomotives ard 74xx (and later 57xx) class 0-6-0 Pannier tanks.

D. J. Lowe Archive

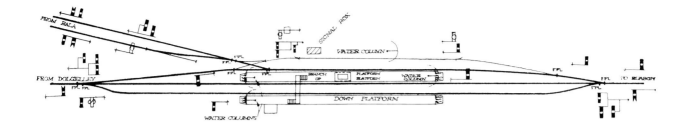

BALA JUNCTION

LLANDDERFEL TO BALA JUNCTION

The line continues to follow the river for most of the three and a half miles to Bala Junction, deviating away from it to cut through a rocky bluff which was tunnelled for 157 yards. Llandderfel tunnel is about half way between the two stations. The gradient is very slight for most of the length.

BALA JUNCTION

The station was situated twenty seven miles from Ruabon and was the junction for the Bala Town and Ffestiniog line. The station was isolated from any road connection and was never advertised in the public time tables. The only access to the station was by a footpath, on the Down side of the line, which continued to the golf links. The tracks widened to provide four running lines through the junction with three platform faces. Most Up and Down trains used the main platform which was an island structure and contained a Waiting Room, a Ladies Room, a Gentlemens W.C. and urinals. The Down platform could only be used by trains to and from Dolgellau, but was little used. An open footbridge provided passenger access and there was a small shelter close to the footbridge steps. Bala Town and Ffestiniog line trains had to use the Up side platform face. A fourth loop line on the Up side provided running round facilities for the branch train. The signal box was on the Up side and contained 53 levers of which seven were spare. There were four water columns provided, one on the Down platform, one at each end of the island platform which could serve either platform roads, with the fourth column located along the loop line on the Corwen side of the signal box.

The station was under the control of the Bala [Town] Station Master, who travelled between the stations as necessary. He carried tickets and an excess fare pad with him to cater for passengers joining the trains at the junction. The normal staff allocation to Bala Junction was two class 4 signalmen.

There was a short siding off the Branch line where locomotives could stand clear of the junction.

The Down Mails from Chester to Barmouth, which was the first train of the day, travelled through the Junction to Bala Town via the relief line, where it discharged its cargo. Then it was propelled back to Bala Junction along the relief siding, which ran parallel to the main branch line. The Sectional Appendix to the Working Time Table specified that the train then came to a halt at the siding signal at the Junction before proceeding into the branch loop line. It then collected the Electric Train Staff from the signalman and proceeded to Llanuwchllyn.

99. Bala Junction. B.R. Standard Class 4MT 4-6-0 No.**75021**, Barmouth bound with the 7.17am from Ruabon has traversed the Vale of Penllyn and now, via Point No.20., F.P.L. No.19 heads for the 'Back Road' at Bala Junction. On the right the photographer has cleverly included an oft neglected view of the adjacent River Dee together with the sluices. A group of passengers await and a member of the railway staff, possibly the telegraph linesman, walks along the cess towards the oncoming train. Looking ahead to the sleeper crossing beyond the signal box (refer to caption 101) the Station Foreman waits to effect the token exchange, the next section being Bala Junction to Llanuwchllyn.
Photo: Peter E. Baughan.

100. Bala Junction. c.1963. The Bala and Festiniog Railway opened from Bala Junction to Festiniog on the 1st November 1882, and the name-board at the Junction proclaimed : BALA JUNCTION for BALA and BLAENAU FESTINIOG. Forerunner of the fate to befall this most delightful of secondary main lines, the line beyond Bala was closed to passengers from 4th January 1960, and to goods traffic from 28th January 1961. It was only necessary to reduce the size of the board and remove the redundant letters so that the appearance of the truncated sign, with its cast-iron letters and beaded face-board remained steadfastly G.W.R.
Photo: C.L.Caddy.

101. Bala Junction. 12th July 1964. Bala Junction Signal Box. Although the line was doomed and goods traffic was to cease from 2nd November the signal box was still smart and cared for. Observe the neat barge boards at the end of the overhanging eaves, and the entry porch, almost a diminutive signal box itself, the tiny slated roof topped with a finial and decorative valance over the door, coal and mop buckets neatly stacked on the landing. Noteworthy too, the diffuser fitted to the lamp standard beside the walkway at the foot of the steps. Levers No.4, 17, 26, 37, 38, 39 and 50 were spare in the 53 lever frame, and the "Special Instructions" contained many interesting items. e.g. P.76, 1960 Appendix to the Working Time Table. "Freight Trains Coupled Together" Corwen to Bala Junction and Bala Junction to Corwen. Signalmen to confer should the length of combined trains exceed the siding capacity at any intermediate crossing station. *Photo: C.L.Caddy.*

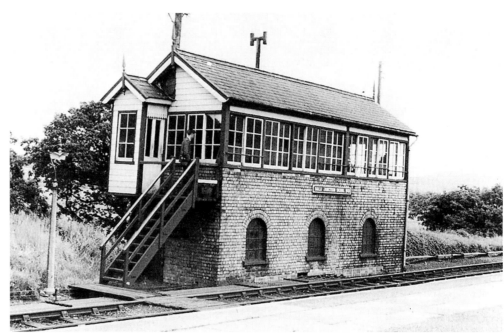

102. Bala Junction. July 1963. High summer and a definitive view of Bala Junction exhibiting that air of (deceptive) somnolence that sometimes fell upon country junctions but was belied by bustling activity when trains arrived from several points simultaneously, and passengers were politely yet rapidly exchanged and directed to their respective destinations. Prominent in the foreground, Down Main Starter Signal, - Lever No.3., is a fine example of the wooden post design, although before the branch closed it was to be replaced by a modern tubular metal post. Of detailed interest is the fitting of cap and finial, details of the signal lamp and spectacle, and the method of fixing the ladder with its safety ring for the protection of the lampman. This is a lower quadrant signal and the arm is slightly above the right angle position. Perhaps the signal wire tension has been adjusted in anticipation of a warm day? *Photo: R.E.G. Read. G.Biddle Collection.*

103. Bala Junction. 7th November 1960. Station Foreman Gwyn Hughes has returned the "Llandderfel to Bala Junction" token to the signal box and the "Train Out Of Section" bell codes will have been exchanged. On the Back Road platform, Station Master Mr.D.G. Edwards confers with Relief Guard Mr.R.G. Jones of Bala. Mr. Edwards was one of three brothers, all Station Masters. Mr.D.G. Edwards served at Trawsfynydd, Bala, Corwen and Acrefair before returning to Bala. His brother Gwilym was at Baschurch, Llangollen, Portmadoc and Welshpool whilst Tegid Edwards was at Rhosllaner-chrugog and Dolgellau. The light engine standing on the Up Main had worked the 4.45am Ruabon to Portmadog goods. Formerly it returned in charge of the 1/12pm passenger train from Barmouth, but when this was withdrawn no other working was available, entailing working as light engine return to Croes Newydd. The elegant footbridge is of a type introduced in the 1880's, Swindon Foundry undertaking the iron-work and the Carriage Shops the joinery. Observe the triangular gusset plate, the G.W.R. monogram, the date - 1884, and in the upper corner, a "Fasces", a design based on an entwined bunch of rods that was the Roman symbol of authority. This airy lattice design of footbridge complements the neo-grecian tracery capping the columns which support the awning, itself an integral part of the composition. The Victorian engineers had a flair for producing work that was visually attractive as well as functionally viable. *Photo: Norman Jones.*

104. Bala Junction. 7th November 1960. [Right] Driver Roy Sharrock brings 2-6-0 No.**6357** into Bala Junction with the 7.50am Birkenhead to Pwllheli (9.27am ex Ruabon).The "Person Appointed" to receive and deliver the token was the Station Foreman, or in his absence the Station Master, so on this occasion Foreman Mr.Gwyn Hughes was waiting for us, behind him a fine display of station "furniture". One, of which immediate advantage was taken, to refill the tea can, was "DRINKING WATER". Note the water crane, the arm supporting brace and the fact that the hose is casually dangling outside the drainage funnel. Behind the hose appears the arm of the Setting Down Post, 78 yards on the Dolgellau side of the signal box. The Picking Up Post was nearer, 58 yards on the Dolgellau side. The splendid three doll Up signal bracket on the curve (of course we see the 'back' side of the signals) was operated by Levers 45, 49 and 52., Point No.35 and F.P.L. No.36. relate. The 'Back' road Down Starter, Lever No.13, is lowered to permit our departure for Llanuwchllyn on completion of station duties. *Photo: Norman Jones.*

105. Bala Junction. 1961. Taken from the footbridge from the Down to the Island platform at Bala Junction, which gives a fine view of the parting of the ways. The left hand line is the main line to Barmouth whilst the right hand tracks lead to Bala Town and Blaenau Festiniog. The 2-6-0 was the workhorse of the Ruabon to Barmouth line, and were to be found working passenger or freight trains from the 1930's until the District was taken over by the London Midland Region early in 1963. With three men on the footplate, possibly the crews were changing over or perhaps someone was refreshing their route knowledge. Note the Pannier 0-6-0PT and one coach which was working the shuttle service to Bala Town. This was all that remained of the branch service to Blaenau Festiniog. The journey from the Junction to the Town station took but two minutes. There were ten journeys Mondays to Fridays in each direction and three extra on Saturdays. *Photo: G.H.Platt.*

106. Bala Junction. c.1963. The main Down platform at Bala Junction looking towards Barmouth. In fact this platform face was rarely used, as may be gleaned from the sparseness of furniture which comprised of a nameboard with a gas lamp close by, a bench seat, the footbridge, a pagoda shelter at the foot of the steps, another gas lamp, a water crane and the Down starter. Most Down trains used the branch platform face. When an Up and Down train to and from Barmouth crossed at the Junction, the branch train to Bala Town would set back from the platform and stand on the relief siding line to Bala until the branch platform was clear when it would pull back into the platform and entrain its passengers. In this view, B.R. Standard Class 4MT 4-6-0 No.**75029** of Croes Newydd (6C) shed pulls into the Up platform with a Class B local from Barmouth to Ruabon. *Photo: C.L.Caddy.*

107. Bala Junction. 1961. Taken from a Down train using the Branch platform face, as was the normal practice. The station presents a tidy face to the public, with the buildings glistening with new paint, and reflects the pride taken by the station staff in their environment. Not a scrap of litter anywhere! Beyond the nameboard is a platform trolley and a double seat. Note the milepost in the foreground, indicating that point is $26\frac{1}{2}$ miles from Llangollen Line Junction. Notice also the tall lamps used to illuminate the steps on the footbridge. A couple of figures stand under the canopy whilst a station official talks to the train crew in the distance. *Photo: G.H.Platt.*

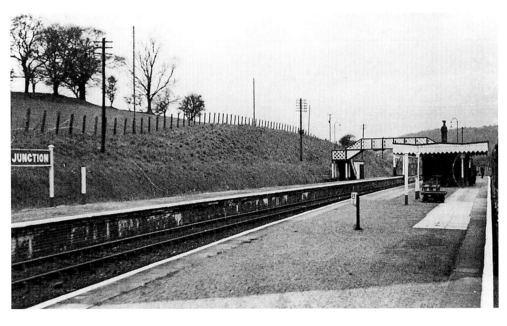

BALA [Town]

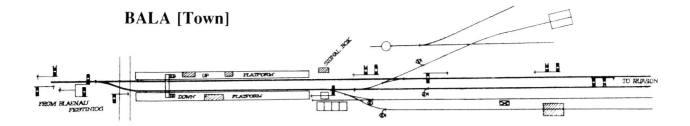

BALA

Bala Town station was 56 chains from Bala Junction and located on the eastern edge of the town, at the commencement of the branch to Ffestiniog. On leaving Bala Junction station the line crossed the river Dee over a two span bridge. Although two tracks extend from the Junction to the Town station, they comprised a single track main line worked by Electric Token between the two points, and a parallel Relief line which enabled movement between the two points without the need to draw a Token from the instrument. Specific operating conditions to working over the Relief line were set down in the Sectional Appendix to the Working Time Table, which enabled non passenger carrying trains, in particular the early morning Mail, to proceed to Bala Town and propel the train back to the junction under the control of the Bala Junction signalman who was assisted by the shunter, who supervised the movements at the Town end.

The station consisted of two passenger platforms, goods yard and siding accommodation and a Locomotive Department. The station buildings were built of brick and were located on the Down side and comprised a Booking Office, Parcels Office, General Waiting Room, Ladies Waiting Room, Porters Room, 2 Lavatories and a Stores Room. A water column was located at the Ffestiniog end of the platform. The Up platform merely provided a shelter. Passengers crossed the line by an open footbridge. The signal box was located on the Up side but a separate ground frame at the Junction end of the station, locked by a key on the Bala-Bala Junction Electric Train Staff gave access to the relief road.

Siding accommodation on the Up side consisted of the Relief line, which could hold 110 wagons, but of necessity was required to be clear at the end of the days work, and No.1. siding which could hold 18 wagons. A load gauge was located over the Relief road. On the Down side, three sidings could hold 41, 33 and 20 wagons respectively. Accommodation for dealing with Horse and Cattle traffic was provided here whilst No.1. siding had a truck weighbridge. A goods warehouse was on the Down side, which contained a crane inside the building. The front of the warehouse was built of stone and was castellated at the request of the owner of a nearby estate, who was opposed to the construction of the railway. The yard contained a crane with 3 ton capacity and there was a cart weighbridge in the mileage yard. The locomotive depot was on the Up side on the Junction side of the station. It comprised two locomotive sidings with an additional turntable siding.

In 1924 the station staff comprised a Station Master [Class 2], 2 Clerks, 1 Junior Clerk, 5 Goods Guards, 2 Shunters, 2 Signalmen, 2 Porter Signalmen, a Station Foreman, Checker, Parcels Porter, and a Porter. The Station Master also controlled Bala Junction and there were two additional Class 4 signalmen based there. On top of this were the staff of the Locomotive Department. Receipts for the year amounted to £13,643, more than half of this coming from Goods receipts. Principal freight traffic dealt with was coal, general merchandise and timber.

108. Bala. c.1950. Bala, viewed from the footbridge, with a train for the Junction about to leave. The coaches are in the livery variously described as carmine and cream, red and yellow or crimson lake and custard, according to one's feelings concerning the changes introduced after the 1948 nationalisation. However, following much comment and public pressure, by 1954 and starting with coaches for the named trains, the popular chocolate and cream livery was re-introduced. Features of the layout mentioned in the text can be identified, particularly in this and the following photographs. Prominent on the right is the castellated front elevation of the 38 ft long stonebuilt goods warehouse. This particular form of construction was adopted to placate Mr Price of Rhiwlas, a local landowner with an estate on the Ffestiniog road about a mile from the station and who had objected to the intrusion of the railway upon the landscape. *Photo: Author's Collection.*

109. Bala. 31st May 1963. A south facing view of 0-6-0PT No.**4683** running round a train of three coaches on the Down line, comprising its own coach and two that were detached from the 7.17am from Ruabon at the Junction. Note the cattle loading dock, pens and siding at the end of the Down platform. The cleared signal adjacent to the signal box was operated by Lever No.25, Lever No.23 referring to that opposite on the Down side. The Station Master is passing the open-fronted cycle shed adjacent to the "gents", which is also the fire assembly point. Note also the fire buckets, one of which will contain sand, the other water. The water tap and hose/hydrant box is on the wall close by. In the distance, an Ivatt Class 2MT 2-6-0 stands in the goods yard whilst a van can be seen inside the castellated goods shed.
Photo: Peter E. Baughan.

110. Bala. c.1957. Halcyon days at Bala station, modernised with electric fittings on reinforced concrete and tubular metal posts, otherwise maintaining its Edwardian aspect. The lady with a child in its perambulator chats to a friend in the Festiniog train whilst 57xx Class 0-6-0PT No.**9793** allocated to Croes Newydd (84J) shed waits in the Up platform with the shuttle to Bala Junction. In traditional footplate fashion, the engine crew chat with colleagues, possibly a weighty conversation, maybe about Local Departmental Committee matters, who knows, as the fireman, with arms folder across his chest lowers his head in deep thought. *Photo: C.L.Caddy.*

111. Bala. 31st May 1963. The rusticated masonry buildings of Bala (Town) Station with their steeply pitched roofs, and gables, were built four-square to withstand the hard winters and blizzards experienced before "global warming" became a meaningful phrase. Particularly noticable in this station approach view is the discoloured appearance of the stonework, yet one would hardly associate Bala with industrial smog but we are advised that such was the case. The area was subject to periods of heavy, persistent mist or fog, which combined with the emissions from the gas works. The sulphuric acid content of the smog was so high that the fabric of the buildings was flaking away, and this phenomenon can be observed on the gable end above the pilaster and cornice close to which the Morris 1000 Traveller with its Cheshire registration plate is parked.
Photo: Peter E. Baughan.

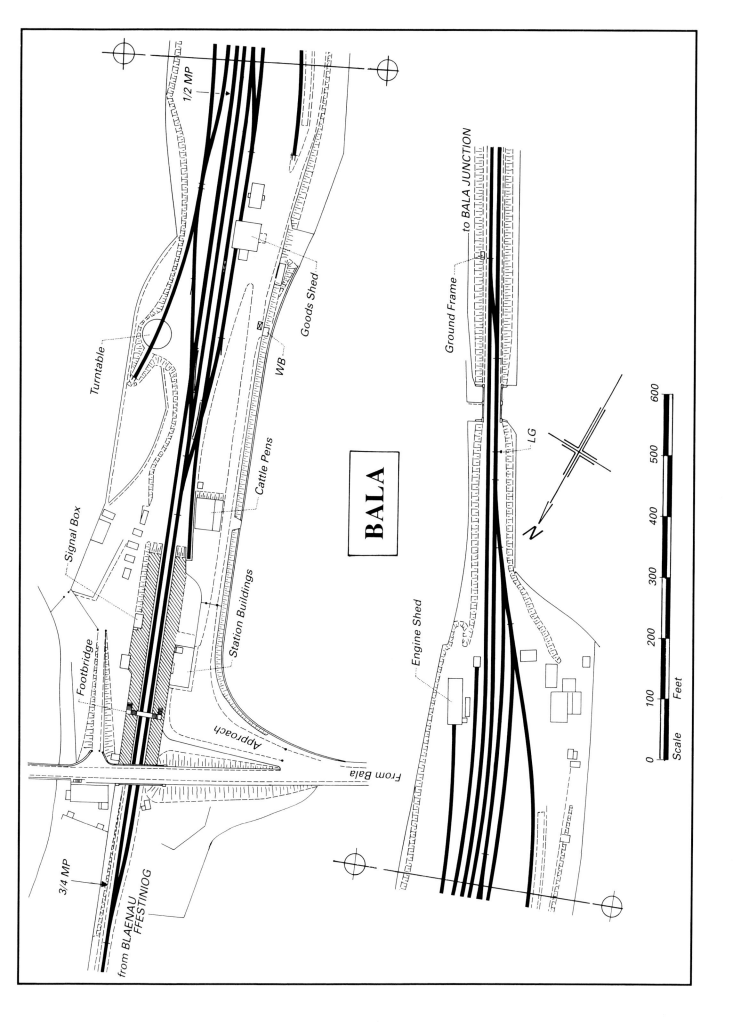

BALA

112. Bala. 31st May 1963. The two coach shuttle service from Bala Junction drawn by 0-6-0PT No.**4683** travelling bunker-first has uncoupled from the stock and run forward onto the remains of the single track to Festiniog, which extended for a bout one hundred yards for operational purposes. The loco will then run through the Up side loop and platform road before setting back on the stock in the down platform. The signalling is unaltered. Partly obscured by the hose of the water crane the column of the Down Main Starter, Lever No.2. To the left of No.4683 appears the reverse side of the two doll bracket signal protecting the Down/Up lines, the taller arm being the Up Main, Lever No.26., the lower Lever No.24. Worthy of note on the extreme left are some aspects of the footbridge. The stringers are of heavy rolled steel joist to which the plating is secured by round head rivets. The verticals to the landing are of steel channel, with substantial bracing struts and strong gusset plates also rivetted in.
Photo: Peter E. Baughan.

113. Bala. 31st May 1963. Bala station after the closure of the Festiniog branch remained as smart, and as well cared for as before, with immaculate platforms, copings gleaming white, well trimmed hedges and spruce, neatly uniformed staff. The Down main platform, on which the Booking Office and most other facilities were situated, hosted the service to Bala Junction. The fireman of 0-6-0PT No.**4683** has removed the tail lamp, which now stands at his feet as he engages in conversation, from the last coach, which has now become the leading vehicle, the engine having run round on the "Up" line and set back onto the coaches. *Photo: Peter E. Baughan.*

114. Bala. c.1957. 0-6-0PT No.**8791** on a one coach working stands at the Down platform with the 3/20pm from Bala to Trawsfynydd, arriving there at 4/25pm and made a connection with the 4/25pm from Blaenau Ffestiniog at 4/53pm. This Down journey was principally for Bala Grammar School children returning home although the general public also made use of it. It arrived back in Bala at 5/34pm and crossed at the Town station with the 5/35pm to Ffestiniog. Note the back of the footbridge, rarely seen, and the buildings on the Up platform. There is a clinical air of cleanliness about the place, with no litter or rubbish tolerated. Just visible beyond the corner of the footbridge support at the far end of the platform is the Up line platform starter and route indicator box below the arm. *Photo: C.L.Caddy.*

BALA JUNCTION TO BALA LAKE HALT

The line from Bala Junction to Dolgellau now changes character, and the easy gradients become undulating with severe climbing to the summit at Garneddwen. The GWR was mindful of this and guards of trains were supplied with keys to enable them to open the occupation key boxes in the sections in case of a failure, a facility which enabled them to contact the signalmen at either end of the respective sections.

On departing from Bala Junction station, the line singled before passing under a road bridge near where the mouth of the river met Llyn Tegid [Bala Lake]. Almost immediately, the site of the original Corwen to Bala terminus was reached.

BALA LAKE HALT

Details of the original formation are unknown to the authors. What buildings accompanied the C.& B. Railway have long since disappeared, with the exception of a house adjoining the site and which was possibly a Station Masters residence. Certainly it was GWR owned and occupied by a company servant until the line closed, when it passed into private hands. Bala Lake Halt came into being in 1934 in a bid to encourage tourists along the line. The station was a very simple affair, comprising a single platform 70ft. in length on the Up side of the track, with a simple shelter and a name board. Passengers crossed a footpath from a

minor road to gain access to the platform, whilst the short length and elongated "S" curve called for Drivers to put their skill and intimate knowledge of the line to the test to ensure that the guards compartment was on the platform. There was no station staff here, the Guards would book passengers to Bala Junction or Llanuwchllyn where they would be re-booked. No lighting was provided at the platform, boarding and alighting the train calling for much vigilance on the part of the Guard. The line passes under a footbridge which gives access to a footpath up into the hillside.

Bala Lake Halt is now the terminus of the Rheilffordd Llyn Tegid, [Bala Lake Railway] a two foot gauge steam operated line established in the 1970s on the original trackbed. The original platform site is utilised, although this was extended in the winter of 1988-89. A run round loop extends the full length of the platform, with spring loaded points at the eastern end set for the loop, whilst the western end of the loop is controlled from a two lever ground frame which is kept padlocked when not in use, and set for the platform line. The key to the frame is kept on the train staff token. An additional siding has been installed at the extreme eastern end of the line connected by a trailing point to the run round neck and which will enable a coach to be parked here at peak times to provide train booking and other facilities.

115. Bala Lake Halt. On a fine summer day, a 43xx Class 2-6-0 locomotive trundles past Bala Lake Halt with the 10.45am Barmouth Junction to Ruabon via Bala Yard. The wheel configuration of these engines and their tractive effort of 25,670 lbs. calculated at 85% of their 200 lb/sq in. boiler pressure put them in Power Class D and Route Category Blue, displayed on the cab sides. Observe the characteristic stance of the footplate crew, the fireman wearing his overall braces over his jacket in traditional G.W.R. fashion. On the Down side of the track is a platelayers hut constructed of used sleepers and slate roof, again in traditional style and making full use of surplus materials irrespective of their original use. Ahead of the locomotive and on the Down side is the fixed distant signal for Bala Junction. The locomotive will be coasting towards the Junction from this point. *Photo: Speed Publications.*

116. Bala Lake Halt. 31st May 1963. The reverse curvature of the line at Bala Lake Halt is evident in this eastward facing view. In the haze of the middle distance, note the overbridge which carried a footpath across the railway. The short platform length and the very basic shelter, coupled with the somewhat isolated location was an indication that regular passengers were somewhat scarce although from July 1935 until the outbreak of War the Halt was sometimes used on summer Sundays by advertised excursion trains as an alternative setting down/picking up point to Bala Town, thus avoiding opening the branch. Great skill was required of drivers to stop with the Guard's coach at the platform, particularly when the light was fading. Today the embankment sides have substantial growth on them.
Photo: Peter E. Baughan.

Bala Lake Halt slumbers in the sunshine on 14th June 1962. Dating from 1934, it was one of the many wayside Halts the GWR introduced on their system around this time, in order to attract tourists along the line. It was a very simple affair with just a shelter and name board to accompany the short platform. Access was via a footpath across the fields and a footbridge from where this picture was taken from.

D. J. Lowe Archive

BALA LAKE HALT TO LLANGOWER

The line between Bala Lake Halt and Llangower hugs the lake on the Up side, and a minor road keeps close company all the way. A severe curve faces drivers on departure as the line enters a small cutting and passes under the minor road bridge. The line runs a few feet above the level of the lake, and in times of flood, some erosion of the track bed has taken place. The narrow gauge line has created an additional halt at Brynhynod about a mile and a half from Bala Lake Halt, at the site of an occupation crossing providing access to the lake side which has developed, and is now a popular picnic area with a small copse of trees providing some shelter.

LLANGOWER HALT

This 70 foot long platform was located on the Down side, and opened in 1929. The platform consisted of sleeper edging with clinker infill. A corrugated iron shelter was provided, which faced the lake, and in winter months passengers were likely to receive spray blown off the lake which did nothing to encourage traffic. The statutory name board was provided, and because Llangower had a few houses close by, was provided with a long burning oil lamp which was attended to by Llanuwchllyn staff, although Guards of trains were utilised to light and extinguish the lamp. Access to the platform was by footpath across a field from the same minor road that accompanied the line. The station was unstaffed, but remained in use until services ceased in 1965. The shelter was removed to Bala Lake Halt by the narrow gauge railway and the platform gradually disintegrated. Some of the clinker infill was also removed to Bala Lake Halt.

Bala Lake Railway did not make use of the platform when it commenced services, but constructed a new halt to the west of the GWR station. Llangower is used as a crossing point, and is unusual in that it consists of two platforms, both on the Up side [or lake side] of the track bed, straddling an occupation crossing.

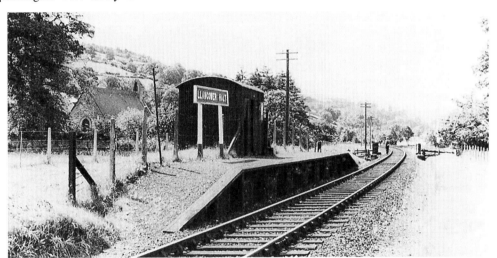

117. Llangower Halt. 12th July 1964.
Llangower Halt followed the pattern of providing very basic, but adequate accommodation. The platform was located on the Down side and had a full size nameboard, with all the standard trimmings, supported on a pair of regulation pattern cast-iron posts. The platform itself consisted of sleeper edged face with cinder infill. The Class A (Pagoda) type of shelters were not installed anywhere between Llangollen and Dolgellau, to our knowledge, and the corrugated-iron shelter at Llangower was, rather unusually, fitted with a door and an end window, one pane of which has been broken. Two lamp posts were provided from which the long-burning lamps could be suspended. Access to the station was by a footpath over a field from the village. The platform and shelter faced the lake which was a short distance away, and in the winter months, spray blew off the lake and into the faces of the waiting passengers. *Photo: C.L.Caddy.*

118. Llangower Halt. 31st May 1963.
British Railways Standard Class 4MT No.**75009** of Croes Newydd (89B) shed approaches the diminutive platform with the 9.27am Ruabon to Barmouth train comprising of three coaches and two vans as tail traffic. The guard looks out of his compartment in the last coach to see if any passengers are waiting at the Halt. Llangower Halt was equipped with a post and fitting originally intended for a long burning oil lamp, but latterly supporting - when required - a "Tilley" pressure lantern. When the Bala Lake Railway commenced operations from Llanuwchllyn to Llangower, they built a new platform and run round loop a quarter of a mile west of the former Llangower Halt, and close to a small car park. The former platform was excavated out and the infill used elsewhere on the narrow gauge line.
Photo: Peter E. Baughan.

Llangower Halt looking westwards. Note the clean and tidy appearance of this little halt, even down to the provision of the portable steps the guard would no doubt use on frequent occasions to aid passengers getting on and off the trains stopping here. Bala Lake is to the right and is also visible in the far distance. A July 1964 view. *D. J. Lowe Archive*

No.**75009** skirts the shores of Lake Bala with a Barmouth to Ruabon passenger train one August day in 1964. Note the Life Belt in its little wooden surround standing near the shoreline of the lake (just to the right of the loco buffer beam). *D. J. Lowe Archive*

LLANGOWER TO FLAG HALT

The line continues to keep close company with the lake although the gradient increased slightly and the line moved a short distance inland.

FLAG HALT

This was built as a private halt for Sir Watkin Williams-Wynn whose home was at Glanllyn across the lake. Sir Watkin was a Director of the original Company and retained powers to stop trains at the halt . A small landing stage was located on the lake close by. A railway owned cottage is on the Down side of the track and guests of Sir Watkin Wynn travelling to and from the house could summon a boat from the halt by the raising of a flag on the platform, hence the name. The halt, which was on the Up side of the line was opened at the same time as the line and survived until the end. The original platform was constructed of wood, was of low height and of short length. It was renewed with stone facing and edging, a raised extension being added later. It was an unstaffed halt with the usual arrangements of excess booking to Bala Junction or Llanuwchllyn prevailing. Originally, there was a crossing and signals located here controlled from a ground frame, but were rarely used and the crossing was taken out and the signals fixed in the "off" position which caused inconvenience to Sir Watkin. It was subsequently arranged for a woman who lived in the cottage to operate the signals as required, for which she was paid 2/- [10p] a week. The shelter on the platform was of unusual appearance, comprising of a timber structure with its back to the lake divided into two open fronted cubicles faced with half round timber giving it a ranch appearance. A nameboard and lamp provided the only other furniture. In 1950 this was renamed Glan Llyn, probably to coincide with the opening of the Urdd Gobaith Cymry centre across the lake at Glanllyn house which the organisation had acquired. The halt still stands and is used occasionally, but as there is no road access, any intending passengers have to walk along the lake shore. The station came under the authority of the Station Master at Llanuwchllyn.

119. Glan Llyn Halt. 26th June 1958. An eastward facing view. A Working Time Table entry recorded "Mileage from Llangollen Line Junction 30m. 14$^1/_4$ch. Glan Llyn Halt". The G.W.R. Chester Division Appendix to the No.14 Section of the Service Time Table (when GLAN LLYN was still FLAG STATION) stated: "Distribution of Weekly Notices. How Notices to be sent. Llanuwchllyn Stationmaster to give to Guard of train to throw out. Method of dealing with receipt. Receipt to be telephoned to Llanuwchllyn Stationmaster". The name was changed from Flag Station to Glan Llyn in 1950. Apart from the ramp at the Llanuwchllyn end, the platform including the raised extension still stands to this day, although the station is now a conditional halt for the Bala Lake Railway. *Photo: Norman Jones.*

120. Glan Llyn Halt. 12th July 1964. Note in this view west, the original low platform and the rather unusual buildings. We have not discovered by whom, or why they were built in this way but the design and execution was, shall we say, original. Constructed of tongue & grooved timber on a wooden frame, the shelter was roofed with corrugated iron sheeting and the front faced with sapling poles which imparted a "Wild West" appearance. There were two sections, one side an open fronted shelter and the other a lock-up section which in Sir William Watkin Wynn's day may have been a parcels office. Inside the shelter were two platform seats and a large framed notice screwed to the rear wall "BRITISH RAILWAYS - GENERAL NOTICES - REGULATIONS AND CONDITIONS". *Photo: C.L.Caddy.*

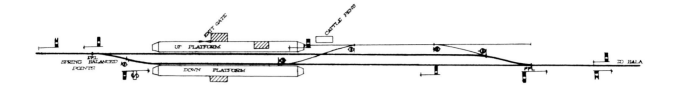

LLANUWCHLLYN

FLAG HALT TO LLANUWCHLLYN

Two hundred yards beyond Flag halt is Pentre Piod occupation crossing where a halt has been established by Bala Lake Railway. A field, which separates the railway line and the lake is used as a camping site, and provides the narrow gauge line with some traffic in peak season. A quarter of a mile further on sees the first real change in gradient, when the climb stiffens to 1 in 70 for approximately half a mile. This was a minor inconvenience for westbound standard gauge trains, but the narrow gauge locomotives can experience difficulties in wet weather with their limited weight and tractive effort. The climb is absolutely straight and from the footplate at the foot of the slope, the task looks formidable. Nevertheless, very rarely has a train stalled on the ascent unless there have been unusual or unforseen circumstances prevail. Just before the summit, an un-classified road to a farm crosses the line and is screened by trees and a high hedge on either side of the road which makes visibility very limited. Despite whistling up for the crossing, the road users do not seem to be aware of the approaching train and some near misses have been reported causing train crews to change colour, and when the situation eases, invoke language which is best left to the imagination. Once over the summit, the line continues in a straight line to Llanuwchllyn. The standard gauge located a fixed distant signal just beyond the crossing, with the platform loop located on the Down side. There were five Occupation key boxes between Bala Junction and Llanuwchllyn which came under the group 1 classification, and thus spaced approximately three quarters of a mile apart.

121. Llanuwchllyn. September 1963. Llanuwchllyn beneath a nicely graded sky. The Up side roof repaired with lead flashing, the same method as used on glazed panes of glass at Ruabon. An unusual feature of the Down side awning is that the roof has a decided fall to the front and that all-round gutters were required. The fitting of the gulley-traps and down spouts near the nicely clipped bush is noteworthy. It seems that at some time modifications had been carried out because the differing ends of the awnings, that nearer the camera being solidly built up, excepting for the saw-tooth edging, whilst the further end features the cut-out fret type of finish with spaces between the end boarding. At the east end of this platform is a corrugated-iron lamp room, whilst an empty coal wagon stands on the Up siding, although this is an older type of wooden bodied end-tipping vehicle. In the far distance the signal, Lever No.17 controls the entrance to the single line. *Photo: R.E.G.Read. G.Biddle Collection.*

LLANUWCHLLYN

Originally called Pandy but subsequently renamed in the early GWR days, Llanuwchllyn was a crossing station. The main buildings were on the Up side and consisted of a Booking Office, General Waiting Room, Ladies Waiting Room, 2 Lavatories and a Store Room. The Down platform had a small brick building which housed a General Waiting Room. A signalbox stood on the Up platform, housing a 20 lever frame which controlled all connections. A water column was provided at the Bala end of the Up platform and the Dolgellau end of the Down platform. There was a loop siding with loading bank on the Up side which could house 30 wagons. Cattle pens were provided off the goods loop adjoining the platform. A load gauge was located over the siding and there was a cart weighbridge in the yard. A small goods warehouse stood alongside. The Station Master was also in charge of Flag Halt, Llys Halt and Garneddwen Loop and signal box. In addition to the Station Master, there were two signalmen at the station and an additional signalman at Garneddwen, a Porter Signalman and 3 Gatewomen attached to the station although the Gatewoman at Rhydydrain Crossing was withdrawn in 1925.

Llanuwchllyn was an Electric Token Exchange Station and the Down direction section was from Llanuwchllyn to Drws y Nant. The instruments were located in the signal box. Garneddwen Loop was located between the two stations and could be switched in as required. The section between Llanuwchllyn and Garneddwen was worked by Electric Train Staff whilst the Llanuwchllyn to Drws-y-Nant section was worked by electric token.

With the development of the Bala Lake Railway in 1972, Llanuwchllyn became the headquarters of the narrow gauge line, and additional buildings were erected to house locomotives and carriages. Modifications and additions to the station buildings were effected which included the installation of a platform canopy that had first been used at the original Cambrian station at Pwllheli. However, when a new station was opened in 1909, the old building was dismantled and the canopy moved to Aberdovey.

122. Llanuwchllyn. c.1963. Croes Newydd Standard Class 4MT 4-6-0 No.**75023** working a Class B train comprised of four ex L.M.S. coaches coasts into Llanuwchllyn station. The injector is blowing through, but no doubt the fireman is preparing to drop the token on the catcher just visible on the right hand edge of the picture. Note the loading gauge beyond the goods warehouse with the van beyond. There was a steady flow of goods traffic for the district and part of the warehouse was let to a local farming co-operative who stored grain and feed there. There were cattle pens in the yard and until the line was closed provided regular livestock traffic into and out of the yard. The safety valves are lifting slightly, and no doubt the half mile climb of 1 in 70 from the lake side to the station livened up the fire and contributed to this state. *Photo: C.L.Caddy.*

123. Llanuwchllyn. 1964. Taken from the eastern end of the Down platform and looking across to the Up side, this view shows the 20 lever signal box with the main station buildings beyond. Notice the ladder of the Up starter, painted white for a third of its height to aid visibility in the dark. The buildings and the fences are freshly painted although the line is under sentence of closure at the time of the taking of this picture. Note that the main building is devoid of a canopy, although the Down shelter possesses one. The whole station is a model of cleanliness and even the shrubs are clipped. A three coach train stands in the Down loop the last coach an ex G.W.R. bow roof vehicle. A solitary passenger awaits the arrival of an Up train which has been signalled. The station has survived and is now the headquarters of Rheilffordd Llyn Tegid, or Bala Lake Railway, although the main building on the Up platform has been enlarged and enhanced by the addition of a canopy, the signal box remains unchanged. *Photo: G.H.Platt.*

124. Llanuwchllyn. October 1963. On the Down platform at Llanuwchllyn, Signalman John Roberts awaits the arrival of L.M.S. Standard Class 2MT 2-6-0 No.46508 with the 1/13pm Ruabon to Barmouth. Beside John on the platform are the lighted "Tilley" lamps, which have replaced the revered "long burning oil lamps", the maintenance of which required almost clinical care and skill to ensure a clear, bright flame that would not smoke to high heaven when left to its own devices. These Tilley's were to be collected by the guard of the incoming train, who would leave one lamp at Llys Halt and the other at Garneddwen Halt, suspending them from the lamp posts on the platforms. Later, they would be collected by the guard of the last train, the 6/45pm from Ruabon to Barmouth and left at Drws-y-Nant, to be picked up the following morning by the guard of the 7.18am from Barmouth and taken back to Llanuwchllyn, so that the procedures could be repeated. *Photo: Norman Jones.*

125. Llanuwchllyn. c.1963. As mentioned in the text, the train workings were not balanced and this picture depicts one of the four Up passenger workings waiting at Llanuwchllyn with a Bala Junction and Ruabon turn. In the left foreground is the Down Setting Down Post, located 52 yards on the Bala Junction side of the signal box. The distance between the two sets of token exchange apparatus was usually 20 yards, so the Picking Up Post is placed at 32 yards from the signal box, and between the two sets of posts, the corrugated-iron sheeted lamp cum store-room with end window. The B.R. Standard Class 4MT 4-6-0 engine, No.75006 was previously allocated to Tyseley Shed (84E). Note the two parachute water tanks, one on each platform, and the new ballast in the cattle dock siding. The Down starter is pulled off indicating that a Barmouth train is due. The Ruabon train has drawn past the Up starter, and probably topped up the water in the tender tank whilst awaiting the token.
Photo: C.L.Caddy.

126. Llanuwchllyn. October 1963. Whilst at Llanuwchllyn, L.M.S. Standard Class 2MT 2-6-0 No.46508 waits for the passage of the 2/35pm Barmouth to Ruabon and Chester train, seen approaching with Standard Class 4MT 4-6-0 No.75025, a Croes Newydd engine in charge. The fireman of No.46508 is preparing for the climb to the summit at Garneddwen, the safety valves lifting as he mounts the tender to pull coal down onto the firing plate. On the Up platform, Tilley lamps wait to be collected by the guard of the Up train and will be dropped off, one each at Glan Llyn and Llangower Halts. They will be collected by the guard of the last train, the 7/15pm from Barmouth to Chester and dropped off at Bala Junction, to be returned to Llanuwchllyn next morning on the 7.03am from Wrexham. Tilley's are pressure vapourising lamps emitting a brilliant light through incandescent mantles.
Photo: Norman Jones.

LLANUWCHLLYN TO GARNEDDWEN LOOP

On leaving Llanuwchllyn, the line is on a rising gradient of 1 in 63 as far as Garneddwen which is the summit. The line passes through bleak open countryside beyond Llanuwchllyn, and the provision of key boxes at frequent and regular intervals was no extravagant luxury. It was not unknown for trains to stick on either side of Garneddwen in winter and pilot engines were available at short notice at Bala and Penmaenpool. In some cases, these engines were attached at Dolgellau and worked to Llanuwchllyn as part of their regular duties usually working back attached to a west bound train.

LLYS HALT

This halt was opened in 1934 and comprised a single platform on the Down side, 70ft. in length and comprising the usual timber edged platform, rudimentary shelter, nameboard and paraffin vapour lamp. The station came under the control of the Llanuwchllyn Station Master with the guard responsible for passenger fares to the next staffed station and the collection of tickets for passengers alighting. As with many of the small halts, no parcels or goods traffic was handled.

A minor road crossed the line here which had a fair density of traffic passing over. The wife of a company servant who lived in the adjoining cottage acted as gate-woman and attended to the crossing gates which were worked by hand. For these duties she received a wage of 4/-d in 1924 plus a bonus of 3/6d. Warning discs were provided in the cottage.

A second road level crossing was located at Rhydydrain which was also attended to by the widow of an employee who lived in the adjoining cottage. The crossing was provided with two gates and a disc was fixed in the cottage. This road led to the mountain and the crossing was used mainly by farmers taking flocks of sheep to and from the high ground. However, Up trains experienced sighting problems as the line was on a curve at this point, and the decision to withdraw the gatekeeper was deferred until 1925 when the crossing keeper was withdrawn.

127. Llys Halt. 31st May 1963. The gradient which faced B.R. Standard Class 4MT 4-6-0 No.**75009** climbing from Llanuwchllyn has eased to 1 in 126 as the Ruabon to Barmouth train nears Llys Halt. A substantial house was provided for the lady crossing keeper and adjacent to the crossing which was at the Dolgellau end of the single platform. The gate can be seen centre right against the hedge. The crossing was on the G.W.R. Bala to Dolgelley Omnibus Telephone Circuit, the call sign for the crossing was 3-1.
Photo: Peter E. Baughan.

128. Llys Halt. c.1960. Llys Halt looking east from the level crossing. The name board again was of regulation pattern but raised on square section wooden posts. Beside the simple concrete, slab sided, and corrugated-iron roofed shelter, note the mounting block and post for the "Tilley" lamp to be placed after being sent up from Llanuwchllyn via the guard of the 1/13pm Down. The crossing-keeper's house was enclosed by the well maintained fencing to the left, and a bi-lingual sign guards the crossing. As at Flag Station, the Station Master at Llanuwchllyn handed copies of the Weekly Notices and Service Books to the guard of a convenient train to throw out to the gate-woman. Acknowledgement of receipt was to be sent to the Station Master by the Ganger.
Photo: Speed Publications.

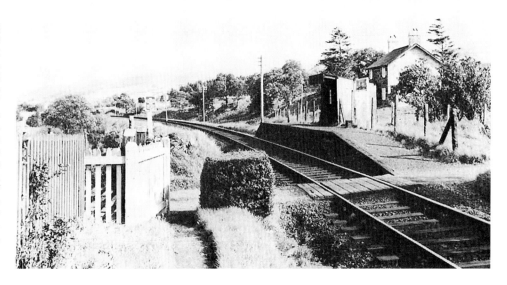

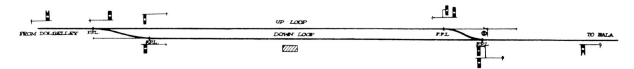

GARNEDDWEN LOOP

GARNEDDWEN LOOP

As previously mentioned, the loop was located just before the summit of the line and was introduced in 1913 for the purpose of shortening the long section between Llanuwchllyn and Drws y Nant. The signal box, which housed a frame containing 22 levers of which six were spare, was located on the Down side of the line and usually only open for eight hours a day. The platforms which were 75 foot long, were provided in the 1930's in an attempt to generate traffic. The faces were staggered and an occupation crossing provided a connection. Apart from the signalmen, there were no staff on duty, and trains that were conditionally booked to stop at the halt were brought into the loop under a red flag displayed to the driver by the signalman, the starting signal being kept at danger. If passengers required setting down the drivers were informed at Llanuwchllyn or Drws y Nant. The signalman on duty was required to telephone the stations on either side for details of the number and class of passengers who boarded at the halt. When the signalbox was closed and passengers wished to board the specified trains,

drivers were instructed to approach the halt prepared to stop. A Ministry of Transport requirement was imposed on the signalman that no train was to be accepted unless there was a clear run into the loop.

When a pilot engine from Dolgellau which had assisted a passenger train on the climb was detached at the loop and was required to return to Dolgellau light engine, a limit of eighteen minutes was imposed for the return working.

Down Freight trains were required to come to rest at a stop board which was located on the Dolgellau side of the Loop box under the standard incline instructions. Similarly, Up Goods trains halted just on the Drws y Nant side of the Garneddwen Loop to pin down brakes prior to descending to Llanuwchllyn. Trap points were located beyond the Up loop on the spur which was worked from the signal box [lever 11 locked by 12] whilst the Down line spring loaded trap was inside the loop at the Llanuwchllyn end.

129. Garneddwen. 24th June 1958. Garneddwen was beautifully situated on the summit plateau ringed by the often cloud-capped circle of Foel Ddu, Foel Fawr, Aran Mawddwy and Aran Benllyn. The Halt was reached by a wicket gate and field path from the Bala to Dolgellau road, crossing the railway by main road overbridge, 34m 43ch from Llangollen Line Junction. On the Dolgellau side of the bridge note the upper portion of the Up Home Signal. Observe to the left of the Down loop Starting Signal (21) and on the right-hand side of the Up line, Signal (19) relating to the "through or single" line when Garneddwen Signal Box was switched out of circuit. Prospective passengers emerging from the field path at a point between the signal box and Key Token Hut and for Up trains crossed over the sleeper crossing to the enclosed path before proceeding to the staggered platform where a passenger shelter was sited at the foot of the ramp. Note the token exchange apparatus near the signal box.

Photo: Norman Jones

130. Garneddwen. 24th June 1958. The view from the summit of the line looking east towards Bala and Ruabon. The lonely and exposed location of the station is apparent in this view, and the isolation is similar to that found on the West Highland and farther north lines in Scotland. The short platform and basic shelter proved adequate for there were very few travellers who made use of the halt outside the summer months. Nevertheless it was the G.W.R.'s policy to provide facilities in the hope that it would encourage trade. Had there been no need for a passing loop at this point it is doubtful whether the halt would have been provided. The signalman had a commanding view in each direction, and traincrews breathed a sigh of relief once they arrived at the summit. The fireman could pull his fire round and tidy up the footplate before taking a well earned rest from his efforts whilst the driver could relax a shade and concentrate on the road ahead. *Photo: Norman Jones.*

131. Garneddwen. c.1960. 4-6-0 No.**7825** *Lechlade Manor* in a rather grimy condition hurries a Barmouth to Chester train of assorted stock through Garneddwen Loop, past the stop board at a little more than the 15 m.p.h. specified for a taken exchange. The fireman will drop the Drws-y-Nant to Garneddwen token in its carrier onto the Setting Down Post (right). The token for the forward section to Llanuwchllyn would be on the picking Up Post 21 yards further east. Particularly noticable is the rampant invasion of undergrowth when comparing this picture with the preceding ones.
Photo: Speed Publications.

132. Garneddwen. 24th June 1958. The definitive photograph capturing the spirit of the Ruabon to Barmouth line. At Garneddwen Loop Signal Box, beneath the shoulders of Maes Gwyn (1538 ft), No.**2204,** a Collett 0-6-0 of the 2251 class drifts by at the prescribed 15 m.p.h. bound for Penmaenpool. The fireman has his arm outstretched in the approved manner to draw out the Hoop and Carrier with the token attached from the Picking Up Post. The procedure was as laid down on Page 42 of the B.R. Western Region Sectional Appendix for October 1960, TABLE D1. ELECTRIC TOKEN RECEIVING AND DELIVERY APPARATUS, illustrated with some splendid detailed line drawings. From the signal box, Signalman Martin R.Jones and Bala Signal and Telegraph Linesman J.C.Freeman maintain a watching brief. *Photo: Norman Jones.*

No.**7824** 'Iford Manor' and 43xx No.**7310**, having crested the summit near Garneddwen, head a Festiniog Railway Society Special towards Drws y Nant and the coast on 22nd April 1961. This area always seemed somewhat remote and desolate for the traveller passing through on a rainy day. Coarse grass is the only available feed for the weather beaten cattle to eat in the field adjacent to the railway line, but the quality of the grass seemingly to offer better grazing prospects for the sheep on the far hillside.

D. J. Lowe Archive

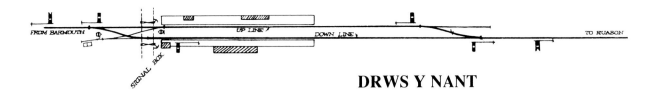

DRWS Y NANT

GARNEDDWEN TO DRWS Y NANT

The descent to Drws y Nant followed the course of Afon Wnion from the summit of the line fairly closely, and the Down goods trains had to proceed with caution. The length of the incline between Garneddwen and Dolgellau was 9 miles 20 chains, with the ruling gradient shown as 1 in 53 to 110.

DRWS Y NANT

Was a crossing station located in a wooded part of the valley and probably one of the most photogenic stations on the entire route. The main buildings were of brick and located on the Down side and comprising a Booking Office, Waiting Room with a Ladies Lavatory and a Gents W.C. and Urinal. A 23 lever signal cabin was located at the foot of the ramp, also on the Down side which controlled the level crossing gates. Wicket gates for passenger access to the platforms were provided on each side, the gate locks being worked from a small 2 lever frame. Passengers crossed the lines at the foot of the ramps at the Dolgellau end. The Up platform contained a Corrugated Iron waiting shed and a matching goods lock up shelter. There was one siding on the Down side, which was an extension of the Down loop beyond the level crossing. The siding access was unusual in that a scissors cross-over enabled movements from the siding to the Up and Down loops to take place. The reason was probably due to the gradient through the station which was 1 in 64 at this point. The siding itself could hold seven wagons and a load gauge stood over the entrance. Horse, cattle and sheep traffic was handled regularly, and a cattle pen was provided. Working the siding called for special instructions to be observed which were set out in the Appendix to the Service Time Tables. Down trains detaching traffic were required to ensure that wagons for Drws y Nant were placed next to the engine. On arrival at the station,

the guard had to ensure that the train was safe and secure before allowing the locomotive to be uncoupled before running forward onto the single line. The wagons to be removed were then allowed to run into the siding by gravity. The locomotive re-coupled and proceeded on towards Dolgellau. An added precaution for Up trains was the provision of a spring loaded Catch Point at the Ruabon end of the Up Loop. Up freight train locomotives with work to do at Drws y Nant were not permitted to be detached from their train.

The station staff consisted of a Station Master and two Signalmen. Passenger receipts in 1924 amounted to only 20% of the total receipts.

One of the regular features until the line closed in 1965 was the working of school childrens trains to and from Dolgellau during term time. Penmaenpool men worked to Drws y Nant ECS in the morning and picked up the children for the Secondary School. The process was reversed in the afternoons.

133. Drws y Nant. 31st May 1963. From the summit at Garneddwen, B.R. Standard Class 4MT 4-6-0 No.**75009** has descended to Drws y Nant with the 9.27am Ruabon to Barmouth train where it will cross paths with the 10.20am Barmouth to Ruabon headed by No.**75006**. In the right foreground is signal No.3 - Up Main to single line - mounted on a wooden pylon-style post. We also observe point 16 with Facing Point Lock (15)(fouling bar) which is worked by the appropriate lever in the box through the rodding and bell crank connections. The action is to raise and lower the bar, since this would be impossible should a train or vehicle be standing over the bar "fouling" it. Operation of the lever, interlocked with other points and signals, "proves" the integrity of the connection. Rule No.232 states that "..... rails, chairs and sleepers ... be .. kept clear of the line and properly stacked, as in the case of the pile of chairs at the foot of the signal post.
Photo: Peter E. Baughan.

134. Drws y Nant. c.1961. The signal box at Drws y Nant was one of the replacements introduced c.1895 and followed closely the design and construction of others installed during the period. The signalman has a good fire going, whilst beyond the level crossing a van stands in the oddly located Down siding. The booking office on the left displays an enamel sign with white lettering on a blue background inscribed "YOU MAY TELEPHONE FROM HERE". Where public call-boxes were not provided this facility rendered a public service in that period when operators still manned many exchanges. The prospective caller told the person in charge of the station the number he wished to contact, which would then be passed to the operator with the comment "A.D.C please". When the caller had finished the exchange would ring back with the cost. (Advise Direct Charge). The procedure sounds complicated but was very simple in practise.
Photo: Speed Publications.

135. Drws y Nant. 12th July 1964. This view, looking east towards Garneddwen and Ruabon gives some indication of the climb ahead for traincrews, and it was not possible to make a 'run' at the bank because of the need to enter the Up loop, exchange single line tokens and pick up and set down passengers. The Up platform was somewhat bare and there was little comfort to be had in the corrugated-iron shelter. Illumination was provided by long burning oil lamps hung on the post by the shelter. Beyond that can be seen the gradient and mileage posts. Accommodation on the Down side was better and the tall chimney indicated that a fire would be burning in the grate during the winter months. Access to the Up platform was across the tracks under the watchful eye of the signalman. One solitary bench seat is provided in front of the building under the shade of a small canopy. *Photo: C.L.Caddy.*

136. Drws y Nant. c.1960. An eastward facing view looking towards Garneddwen featuring XP "fitted" vans in the Down siding. The centre vehicle is a 12 tonner, No.W.145371 and all three carry the I.C.I. "Fertiliser" logo. An up-ended wheelbarrow is propped against the corner wall of the neat mess-hut with its brick chimney and note the splendid grindstone still further right. Ahead of the parked van and motorcycle is a small utility hut, whilst sweeping down towards the station, serried ranks of conifers do little for the rounded mass of Moel Ddu. Notice also the loading gauge with its hinged extensions. Between it and the corner of the van can be seen the Up direction Setting Down Post. The trackwork to the siding is unusual and of special interest.
Photo: Speed Publications.

The mist clings to the mountain sides as BR standard 4-6-0 No.**75009** tackles the climb to Drws y Nant with a Barmouth-Ruabon service in August 1964. Steep gradients (as much as 1 in 50) were encountered as the railway passed through the Cambrian Mountains at this point, and with inclement weather (similar to the day this picture was taken on), the task would have been made the more difficult with a 'greasy' rail to contend with. In 'Duke' and 'Dukedog' days, with a heavy express and in conditions as described, it was a struggle even for two engines to drag a train up the grade near here, with the train speed reduced to a walking pace. As a matter of interest, No.**75009** would be one of three members of its class to survive to the very end of BR steam, some four years after this picture was taken.

D.J. Lowe Archive

DRWS Y NANT TO BONTNEWYDD

At Rhydymain about a mile beyond Drws y Nant, a pedestrian footpath crossed the line. Drivers of trains in each direction were required to sound a warning and so whistle boards were provided. The gradient was still severe and caution was exercised by all Down train drivers due to visibility being restricted for much of the way.

WNION HALT

Located 40 miles from Ruabon, this halt was opened in 1933. It comprised a 50ft. platform on the Up side of the line, the gradient at this point being 1 in 66. The platform was the usual timber edged construction, with an open shelter, nameboard and a paraffin vapour lamp. The guard was responsible for excess booking passengers to Bontnewydd or Drws y Nant. At the western end of the platform, the line passed under a road bridge which made sighting of the platform difficult for drivers during hours of darkness. The halt came under the control of the Bontnewydd Station Master.

G.W.R.

Bontnewydd

137. Wnion Halt. 12th July 1964. That Wnion Halt, as stated in the Working Time Table of Passenger Trains, Shrewsbury District, (Chester Area) Main Line and Branches, 12th September 1960 to 11th June 1961 (or until further notice) was still regarded in London Midland Region days as being 39m 60ch from Llangollen Line Junction, confirmed by the mileage post on the platform. The Halt was a very basic affair but typical of the small structures put up by the G.W.R. in an attempt to boost trade in the 1930's, and apart from the rudimentary shelter, the furniture consisted of a nameboard and a lamp holder. Note the small step by the side of the shelter, which the guard would use to assist passengers alighting and boarding the coach from the low platform. The platform itself was constructed of former sleepers with cinder infill for the platform surface. *Photo: C.L.Caddy.*

138. Wnion Halt. 31st May 1963. B.R. Standard Class 4MT 4-6-0 No.75009 calls at Wnion Halt with a Down Ruabon to Barmouth train. Prominent is the unsophisticated repair to the pine-boarded shelter, where a corner post (centre) has rotted at the foot and been cut off flush with the ground. A new short section has then been inserted below to support the building and fitted with a weatherproof capping. Petty crime was not a problem in rural areas and a bicycle is parked awaiting its owners return. The corrugated-iron shelter roof is extended to form a short awning, complete with valance, whilst between shelter and nameboard we note a lamp-post with "half harp" fitting. Access to the station from the road was down a short footpath, protected by the fence seen behind the guard. *Photo: Peter E. Baughan.*

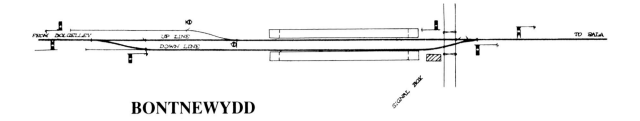

BONTNEWYDD

BONTNEWYDD

Originally, Bontnewydd was a non-crossing station but in 1923 a loop was installed and the station layout remodelled. The descent from Drws y Nant was at its steepest [1 in 50] for the whole line although easing to 1 in 200 in the station loop, and demanding considerable skill of traincrews. A road crossed the line at the station just before the platforms, the level crossing gates being worked from the signal cabin which was on the Dolgellau side of the crossing. A shelter was the only structure on the Down platform, the face of which was built mainly of redundant sleepers, the main buildings being located on the Up side and consisting of a Booking Office, General Waiting Room, Ladies Waiting Room and a Gents WC and Urinal. In addition,

there was a corrugated iron lock up for the storage of goods on the Up platform. There was a single siding, also on the Up side, which could hold 15 wagons. A load gauge was provided there and the goods yard also contained a cart weighbridge. The station Master [Class 5] had a house on the site. The only other staff were two signalmen, their signalbox housing a 20 lever frame. The Electric train Staff sections were to Drws y Nant and Dolgellau. Because of the steep gradient, two catch points were located in the Up Loop and were worked from the box. Most of the revenue before the war came from Goods traffic, and there was a regular supply of timber loaded and carried from the station.

139. Bontnewydd. c.1960. Taken from the level crossing and looking west towards Dolgelley and Barmouth, this view shows the main buildings on the Up platform and the rather basic structure on the Down which was constructed of corrugated-iron. . This station was remodelled in the 1920's when the crossing loop was installed. The buildings on the Up platform date from the opening of the station. For the trains working east towards Ruabon, the gradient was at its steepest just beyond the level crossing (1 in 50) and taxed the skill of traincrews to the utmost, particularly in wet weather. Note the lamp post on the Down platform with a distinct 'lean' towards the tracks.
Photo: Speed Publications.

140. Bontnewydd. c.1964. Being one of the later generation of signal boxes, Bontnewydd was mainly notable for its lapboard construction and larger paned windows, whilst a generously sized sliding window illuminated and ventilated the lower storey which contained the locking frame and stairs to the upper floor. Quite a number of levers were spare, 3, 4, 6, 7, 8, 14, 15 and 16. Notably an oil lamp casing seen being affixed to the right hand corner of the box some twelve months earlier has been removed together with undergrowth from around the base, giving a view of the car park. Obviously the craft of masonry was still practised at Bontnewydd as witness the small bridge, its semi-circular arch built of stones set soldier fashion and apparantly without an obvious keystone.
Photo: Speed Publications.

No.**7827** 'Lydham Manor' and 2-6-2T No.**4555** are seen running through Bontnewydd heading for the coast with the TRPS AGM Special on 26ᵗʰ September 1964. The falling gradient continued here at 1 in 91, so some careful applications of the brakes would be required with this nine coach special before Dolgelley was reached. No.**7827** was running with a 6F shed plate by this time, Machynlleth being its 'home' shed. It would have about another twelve months use before being withdrawn from Shrewsbury depot. The 'Prairie' tank on the other hand was already privately owned and used on official BR duties from time to time. Fortunately 'Lydham Manor' would eventually be saved from Woodhams Barry scrap yard, and now works on another Holiday Line on the Paignton and Dartmouth Railway.

D. J. Lowe Archive

141. Bontnewydd. c.1963. B.R. Standard Class 4MT 4-6-0 No.**75029** of Croes Newydd shed (6C) stands at the Down platform with a Ruabon to Barmouth Class B train. The guard and signalman survey the situation from the platform, and a couple of open carriage doors seem to suggest that there were a few passengers. The train will have coasted down from Drws y Coed and the fireman will have tidied up the footplate. The lifting safety valves indicate that all is well on the engine and it will not be unduly taxed for the downhill run to Dolgellau. Note the sleeper construction of the Down platform. Economy was the watchword when this platform was put in. On the Up side lack of attention to weed-killing is obvious and growth is taking over by the fence posts. The permanent way however looks in excellent shape. *Photo: C.L.Caddy.*

142. Bontnewydd. 31st May 1963. There was almost a "Colonel Stephens Light Railway" aspect to the Down platform, built mainly of redundant sleepers and suffering from subsidence. Observe the massive beams and cross-bracing, making a pier-like base on which the shelter was erected, and the platform, strengthened by a form of flying buttress, engineered from surplus rail, stout right-angled girders and braced with rivetted triangular brackets. The corrugated-iron shelter is in good condition, the rigorous specification to which they were produced ensuring long life for a material which although perhaps looked askance at today, was a typical and useful product of its period. It would be a hardy soul who,patronised the seat on this bleak expanse of platform, especially after dark, although a post and bracket for a long burning oil lamp were provided. *Photo: Peter E. Baughan.*

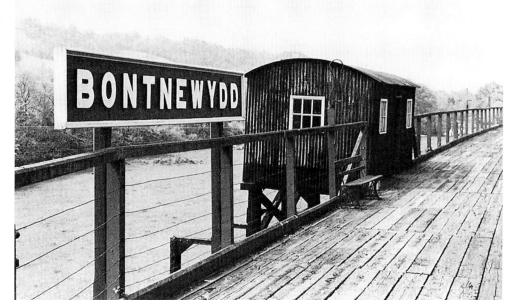

143. Bontnewydd. c.1963. This is an eastward facing view of Bontnewydd and we can see on the Up side another example of the corrugated-iron unit adapted on this occasion as a goods storage shed. With a regard for passenger comfort, it is now obvious that the Down side shelter housed a stove, the vent-pipe, chimney and draught excluding cowl appearing to the right of the end window. The hipped roof of the Up side "main" buildings is laid with tiles or heavy slates in a diamond pattern, ornamented with half-round ridge. The heavy growth of moss outlining the shapes is very noticeable. Similar types of chimney stack have appeared on other stations, but this is the first example surmounted by domestic style "pots". Finally we refer to the sign to the left of the crossing gates which reads "Catch Points". *Photo: C.L.Caddy.*

BONTNEWYDD TO DOLGELLAU

On regaining the single line, the gradient stiffened to 1 in 91 for the next mile as far as Dolserau where a halt of that name was opened on the Up side of the line in 1935. Beyond the platform the gradient eased slightly to 1 in 110 for another mile before the valley widened, changing briefly to an ascending 1 in 117 for a hundred yards or so before continuing the descent at 1 in 213/187/600 into Dolgellau. There were three Occupation Key Boxes within the section [Group 5], Hut numbers 16,17 and 18, each about three quarters of a mile apart.

DOLSERAU HALT

The platform was sufficient to accommodate a single coach and was constructed in the usual economy type method employed on the line - timber edged platform, basic open shelter, lamp and nameboard. The latter was lettered "Dolserau Halt for Torrent Walk", which was a local beauty spot. As usual for the halt, there were no staff in attendance, the guard dealing with any passengers. There was no provision for freight or parcels, this being dealt with from Dolgellau. The Halt opened in 1935 and survived the war and Nationalization but succumbed early to progress, closing in 1951.

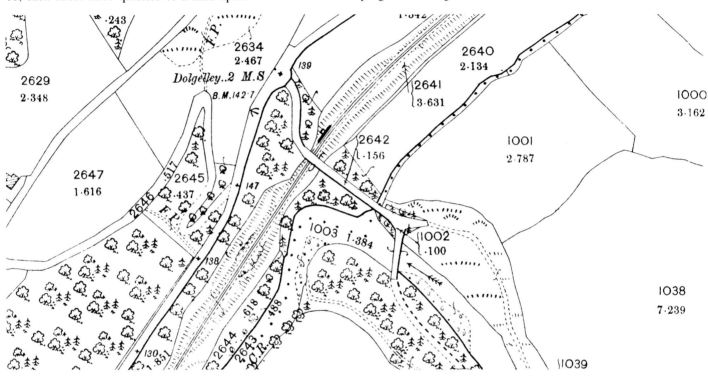

144. Dolserau Halt. *Photo: L.G.R.P.*

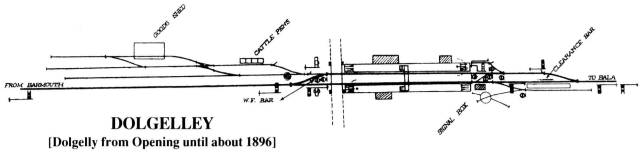

DOLGELLEY
[Dolgelly from Opening until about 1896]
[Dolgellau from June 1960 until closure]

DOLGELLAU

Dolgellau [originally spelt Dolgelly by the promoting Company, was changed to Dolgelley and finally in 1960 became Dolgellau] was the limit of the GWR line from Ruabon, and formed an end on junction with the Cambrian, who had themselves taken over the Aberystwyth and Welsh Coast Railway and constructed the line from Barmouth Junction on the coast as far as Penmaenpool, when shortage of funds prevented the completion of the line to Dolgellau until 1869 after a wait of four years. The GWR buildings were located on the Up side platform and comprised a Station Masters Office, combined Booking and Parcels Office, Ladies Waiting Room, General Waiting Room, Refreshment Room, an Old Footwarmers Room, 2 Lavatories and a Guards Room. The Cambrian buildings were located on the Down platform, and comprised the Cambrian Station Masters Office and Booking Office, General Waiting Room, Ladies Waiting Room and 2 Lavatories. The Cambrian Station Masters and Booking Office were closed upon amalgamation. In addition, the GWR had a house intended for their Station Master. Prior to 1925, passengers crossed the line by walking up steps to the road and down a ramp, but the station building was remodelled and included in the rebuilding was the installation of a footbridge at the Ruabon end of the platform. Before the grouping there were two signal boxes here, one on the Down side of the line, the second on the Up platform although the latter had been taken out of use by 1925 and all points and signals worked from the Down side box, which housed a frame of 35 levers.

A 42ft. diameter turntable was located on the Down side but was rarely used after the Grouping and was taken out of commission before the line closed in 1965. Two water columns were provided, one at the Barmouth end of the Down platform and the other at the Bala end of the Up platform.

Siding accommodation consisted of a Horse Landing at the station on the Up side which could hold 4 wagons. Also on the Up side were three other sidings which could hold 47, 46 and 31 wagons respectively. A Carriage Siding on the Down side held 35 wagons. Two load gauges were provided and there was a cart weighbridge in the Goods Yard. Horse and cattle traffic was dealt with, the latter at pens in the yard. A warehouse in the yard was 56 feet in length with a line passing through it. An internal crane had a capacity of 1 ton and another crane was located in the mileage yard. The local Farmers Co-operative also had a corrugated iron shed where goods were stored and distributed.

In 1924 the staff employed comprised a Station Master Class 2, 2 clerks, and a junior clerk, 2 signalmen, a checker, 2 goods porters, a Passenger guard, 2 Porter Guards, 2 Goods Guards and 2 lad porters. Goods traffic receipts provided sixty percent of the total revenue for the same year. Much of the traffic was general goods, timber and livestock. In the same period, the GWR also ran bus services to Dinas Mawddwy, Machynlleth via Tal-y-Llyn and Corris, and Drws y Nant. These services were eventually taken over by the Wrexham based Western Transport, which was itself taken over by Crosville Motor Services Ltd.

145. Dolgellau. 31st May 1963. From the footbridge we have this view of Dolgellau looking towards Bontnewydd, with signs on the Up and Down platforms stating that "PASSENGERS ARE NOT ALLOWED TO CROSS THE RAILWAY EXCEPT BY THE BRIDGE". The parachute water tank is flanked by two braziers, an empty coal bunker and gas lamp, whilst the bracket supporting signal (2) has an extemporised if robust appearance. Also of note in the Up siding are the Loading Gauge Catch Point (16A) and connection to the main Up line via point 16B, whilst in the loop behind the signal box waits B.R. Standard Class 2MT 2-6-0 No.**78002**, tender leading, with the two coaches comprising the 1/14pm Barmouth train. These were not auto-trains, the engine running round the coaches at each end of the journey. *Photo: Peter E. Baughan.*

146. Dolgellau. 31st May 1963. On the G.W.R. side at Dolgellau, the re-titled name-board is supported on standard posts, straddling an example of the regulation platform seat. The nearer brick-built structure, as befitted this important station, was handsome, with a substantial plinth and tall narrow doors and windows with curved heads. Three rows of dentils compliment a hipped roof, and an exuberant embellishment of chimney stacks crowned with a variety of pots and cowls. Unfortunately, the ornamental cast-iron railings above the ridge tiles have in part rusted away. The awning, with its sheet lead covering deserves attention and the eye is drawn to the graceful tracery of the footbridge. Posters nostalgically advertise "ATTRACTIVE EXCURSION WHIT SUNDAY 2nd JUNE 1963 LLANGOLLEN, DOLGELLAU, BARMOUTH", and "A SPECIAL EXCURSION LLANGOLLEN, CORWEN, BALA, DOLGELLAU AND BARMOUTH". *Photo: Peter E. Baughan.*

147. Dolgellau. September 1963. The passage of four months has seen a change in posters "CHEAP DAY TICKETS from DOLGELLAU" now being on offer, its "running mate" being of a pictorial design. We can observe the architectural differences between the G.W.R. and Cambrian Railways sides. Steeply pitched roofs are common to both, but the former double-pitched type is positioned transversely to the platform face whilst the Cambrian favoured a saddle, or ridge-roofed building parallel to the platform. The latter's chimneys are vaguely Tudor, rising from plinths inset into the ridge tiles, and surmounted by stone capping and a moulded cornice, this feature having been removed from the eastern stack. Note the similarity between this footbridge and that at Bala, although more modern materials were used at Dolgellau. *Photo: R.E.G. Read. G. Biddle Collection.*

148. Dolgellau. September 1963. A low angle and reflected light illuminate the constructional details of Dolgellau's awnings. The heavy Cambrian feature already described is fixed to the supporting columns via a form of chair bolted to the Romanesque capitals. The GWR design was neater with circular columns carrying, horizontally, a steel-channel main-frame with supporting timber cross-beams secured corbel fashion by nicely machined wooden brackets set into the web of the girder. A fine set of iron railings adorns the Down side access ramp and other details along the platform include the racked fire-buckets, platform seat, gas lamp and another venture into classical architecture where two arches pierce the ramp. *Photo: R.E.G. Read. G. Biddle Collection.*

149. Dolgellau. c.1961. 43xx Class
2-6-0 No.**7313** from Croes Newydd
shed (84J) brings an Up freight into
Dolgellau. The signal box to the right
was disused and all connections had
been transferred to that on the Down
side, from which all movements were
now controlled. Class H headcode is
carried denoting a train not running
under C, D, E or F conditions. The
signal box bell code was 1 pause 4 and
the Class H code could also be used for
Auger or Tamping Machines, or Track
Recording Cars not stopping in section
when the bell code was 2-2-3. There
were five other possible variations, all
belled differently.   *Photo: G.H.Platt.*

150. Dolgellau. 31st May 1963. B.R.
Standard Class 4MT 4-6-0 No.**75009**
and train seen from the footbridge at
Dolgellau looking towards Barmouth,
where we note that the banner repeater is cleared, the train about to
leave for Penmaenpool. To the left is
the Afon Wnion and note the cut-
water on the upstream arch of Bont
Fawr. The awning on the right
(G.W.R.) is notable as an example of
the design in which lead sheeting was
affixed to the boarded canopy by flat-
sided, round-topped battens over
which the lead was rolled and when
done skilfully made a decorative and
striking feature. The picture also gives
an interesting view of the G.W.R.
coach roofs, useful to modellers.
      Photo: Peter E. Baughan.

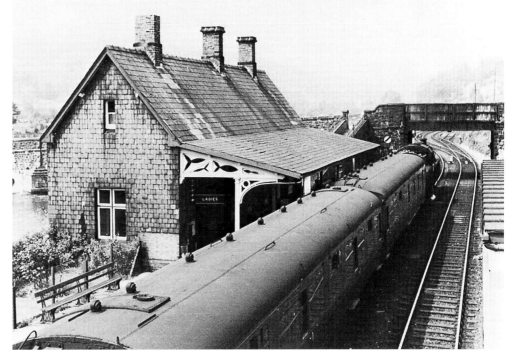

151. Dolgelley. The posters on the
Down, Cambrian, side building at Dolgelley extol the virtues of Brighton and
Hove, as the auto-train comprising the
Barmouth shuttle waits in the platform,
its driver comfortably slumped in his
seat in the driving compartment.
Above his window are the warning
gong and Class B headlight. The regulator was worked by the fireman in the
cab of the propelling 0-4-2T who responded to a code of bell signals from
his driver. A traveller wearing turned
down Wellington boots is surrounded
by hand luggage and sits beside the
ramp. Both platforms are dotted with
passengers whilst an elderly gentleman
surmounts the footbridge to the Up
platform with difficulty. The GWR
started the Dolgelley to Barmouth
service with steam railcars in 1922,
replacing them in the summer of 1927
by auto-trains worked at first by the 0-
4-2T's (517, class) later supplanted by
the 14xx class (originally 48xx class)
introduced by Mr. Collett in 1932.
Some trains ran to Portmadoc or Har-
lech but by the summer of 1947 traffic
was reduced and the local service at the
western end was confined to Dolgelley
to Barmouth except for the Dolgelley
to Drws y Nant school trains.
      Photo: Speed Publications.

ROUTE OF THE
CORONATION
LAND CRUISE
1953

The following brief notes are given to help the traveller identify the principal points of interest on the route. The tour is divided into four sections—Rhyl to Corwen, Corwen to Barmouth, Barmouth to Afonwen and Afonwen to Rhyl. All references are given looking ahead, that is, facing the direction of travel.

SECTION 2—

Corwen to Barmouth

The train stops for a few minutes at Corwen, a small market town where Glendower had his headquarters and where he assembled his forces before the battle of Shrewsbury. Beyond Corwen, the valley of the Dee, which increases in beauty as we ascend, is known as the Vale of Edeyrnion. Passing Bala Junction the peaceful market town of Bala is seen a short distance away to the right, and the train is soon running alongside Bala Lake. The lake ("Llyn Tegid" in Welsh) is 3½ miles long, ½ mile broad, and 530 feet deep, and, with the foothills covered with heather, ferns and scattered trees and the great mountain of Arenig Fawr (2,800 ft.) behind, possesses a singular charm in clear and sunny weather. To our left as we proceed, Aran Benllyn (2,901 ft.) comes boldly into view at the end of its long ridge. The line ascends through a desolate region, overshadowed by Aran Benllyn, to its highest point (770 feet). The descent is rapid to Drws-y-Nant and through the Valley of Wnion, crossing and recrossing the impetuous stream amid some of the most delightful sylvan scenes in Wales. The cliffs of Cader Idris (2,927 ft.), with the steep face of Tyrau Mawr, rise directly ahead to our left as we approach Dolgelley, the capital of Merionethshire. Owen Glendower held a Welsh Parliament at Dolgelley in 1404, and in the following year signed his alliance with Charles VI of France. The town manufactures woollen goods, but is chiefly noted as a tourist resort owing to its singularly beautiful situation. Our route now runs alongside the Mawddach Estuary, with splendid views of the Cader Idris range on the left. The Afon Mawddach is crossed by a long railway bridge, and we arrive at Barmouth, where time is allowed to enjoy the glorious views.

With the Compliments of

BRITISH RAILWAYS

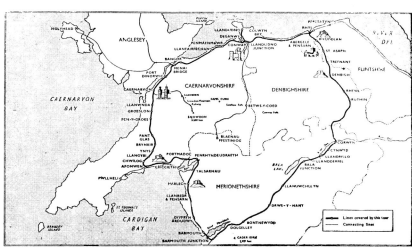

Above and Left: Scaled down reproductions of the leaflet produced for the Coronation Land Cruise of 1953. British Railways renamed the tour for that year in recognition of the Coronation of Queen Elizabeth II. Route and timings were the same as those for the North Wales Land Cruise which at 13/- for the round trip was excellent value. On Mondays to Fridays during the summer season, the tour operated in a clockwise direction from Llandudno via Rhyl, Corwen, Dolgelley, Barmouth, Portmadoc, Caernarvon and Bangor. On Tuesdays, Wednesdays and Thursdays, it ran in the reverse direction, arriving Barmouth at 12.20 pm and allowing a couple of hours for sightseeing. **Below:** Dolgelley was a very convenient centre for tourists and the like and much was done to attract them to the area. The Western Region handbills reproduced here give details of these popular "Holiday Runabout Tickets" available for the respective areas. That to the left shows the front of the 1962 leaflet, whilst that to the right illustrates the rear of the 1958 leaflet. Close inspection will reveal that inflation was also a problem.

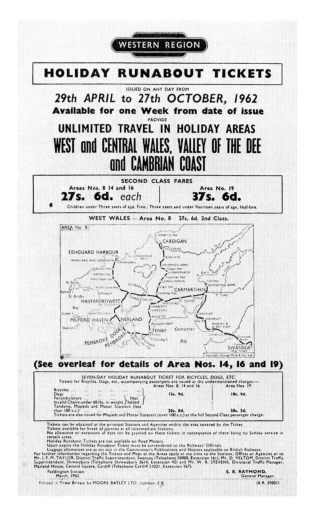

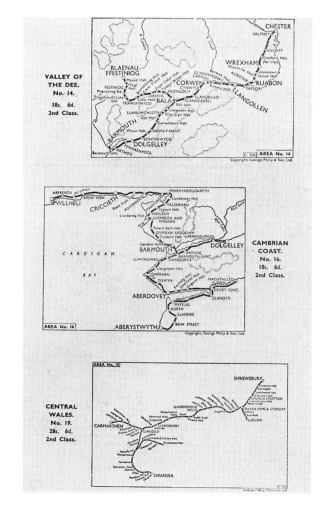

No. **7827** 'Lydham Manor' and 2-6-2T No.**4555** on the TRPS AGM Special are seen entering the Down loop at Penmaenpool on 26ᵗʰ September 1964. The beauty of the Mawddach Estuary, flanked by the mountains at this point can be much appreciated in this view, as the railway line made its way down to Morfa Mawddach, what was formerly Barmouth Junction.

D. J. Lowe Archive

The run into Penmaenpool station, looking towards Dolgelley (Dolgellau), in the August of 1966, just over eighteen months after closure. The line was 'mothballed' at the request of the local Council for two years after it had been closed at the beginning of 1965, to ensure adequate bus services could be provided, and road improvements carried out. This meant that much of this 'sleeping' railway dropped into a time warp with much of the infrastructure and artefacts left in place. Sadly, the demolition contractors arrived in 1967 and subsequently removed everything apart from the signal box, which was to survive to the present day as an RSPB observatory. The toll for crossing the bridge is still collected today!

D. J. Lowe Archive

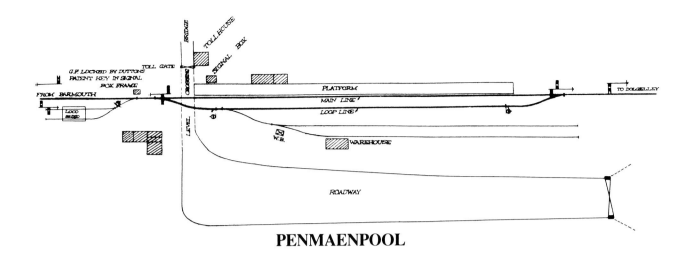

PENMAENPOOL

DOLGELLAU TO PENMAENPOOL

The line continued to fall beyond the station although the gradients encountered were gentle and the river kept company for the next two miles until Penmaenpool was reached. The river widened perceptively, becoming tidal within a mile of leaving Dolgellau and three underbridges within a mile were described as Tidal Culverts.

PENMAENPOOL

Originally, Penmaenpool consisted of a single wooden platform with a General Waiting Shelter for passengers and a small lock up shed, a signal box, a run round loop and two sidings with a capacity of 46 wagons in the yard, which also contained a wooden warehouse. A cart weighbridge was provided. On the Down side was the Booking Office, which contained the block instruments, a General Waiting Room and 2 Lavatories. The public road from Dolgellau to Towyn ran through the Cambrian station approach road across the line on a level crossing and on to a wooden toll bridge across the river. A house was provided

for the Station Master. This sufficed until the Grouping, when the signalbox was replaced. At the time the modifications were being considered, a proposal was made to construct an island type platform, but eventually a wooden platform was installed on the Down side. The station staff comprised a Station Master and two Signalmen. Passenger traffic receipts were slightly better than the Goods receipts in 1924.

A quarter of a mile beyond the station on the Down side was a wooden two road Locomotive shed, with a water tank and column. The points to the shed were controlled by a key, interlocked from the signal box. In 1924, two locomotives and a steam rail car were located here, the latter used mainly on the Dolgellau to Barmouth shuttle. At one time, seven sets of men worked from here but this was reduced as traffic diminished until only four sets remained on closure. After Grouping the shed became an outstation under the control of Croes Newydd. Trains departing on and off shed telephoned the Penmaenpool signal box who released the points.

152. Penmaenpool. c.1925. A nostalgic picture of the single platform on the Up side prior to the mid-1920's alterations, with a nameboard inscribed
PENMAENPOOL
BONTDDU
and for illumination a post mounted oil lamp with magic-lantern style chimney. In the foreground there is a Cambrian style Point Indicator (or Ground Signal), the colour aspects being green and magenta. On the extreme left can be seen a private owner wooden bodied four-plank wagon, the firm being CAWOOD of SALOP, a very well known name of the period. Also in the left distance is the goods shed, and a sleeper enclosure over the top of which protrudes the jib of a hand crane.
Photo: Authors Collection.

153. Penmaenpool. c.1925. Penmaenpool's Down side facilities, Booking Office, General Waiting Room and Station House, in pristine condition. Note the rack of three fire buckets and admire the bonding and pattern of headers and stretchers in which the vari-coloured glazed bricks are laid. A length of diamond embossed tiling forms a fore-court from which rise wooden stanchions to support an extension of the pitched roof which forms an awning. A typical feature of the period was the enamelled sign "VIROL. GROWING BOYS NEED IT". One poster board has been scraped down but the non-colour sensitive plates have not reproduced the lettering on the others - possibly blue on white. The Arthog porter would attend to the long-burning lamps, of which a splendid example appears on the unusual bracket to the right and inside the elegant casing can be seen the domestic-style, glass-chimneyed lamp.

Photo: Authors Collection.

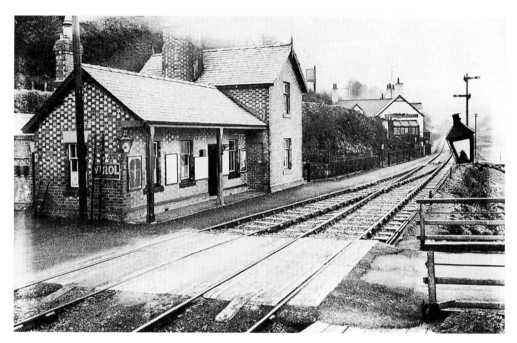

154. Penmaenpool. c.1960. Looking east at Penmaenpool, with the yard deserted except for the radiator of a legendary S.S.Jaguar car. To reach the Down platform from the yard, passengers had to cross the siding line by the sleepered foot crossing, and we note two signs "TO PLATFORM" and "BEWARE OF TRAINS". The small goods warehouse is of a neat and attractive design, and occupying a prominent position is signal 24 and the wagon loading gauge. Penmaenpool closed to freight traffic on 4th May 1964 but although trains no longer skirt the estuary, the signal box remains, bright in chocolate and cream livery. It was reopened in 1976 as an information centre for the Royal Society for the Protection of Birds, at that time their first such centre not sited on a reserve. It was designed by and is managed in conjunction with the North Wales Naturalists Trust at the invitation of Gwynedd County Council.

Photo: Speed Publications.

155. Penmaenpool. 12th July 1964. The locomotive shed at Penmaenpool, a sub-shed to Croes Newydd. Class 2MT Ivatt Taper Boiler 2-6-0 No.**46521** and 4MT 4-6-0 No.**75021**, both carrying Croes Newydd (6C) shed plates seem quite at home in the confines of this former Cambrian/GWR outpost. In the most unfamiliar surroundings the distinctive louvred smoke-vents, and the ever-present haze of simmering locomotives signalled the home of resting engines. Penmaenpool's are a neat version, with miniature hipped and slated roofs embellished with ridge tiles. For the depot, Oswestry produced another of their rectangular water tanks, but unlike that at Dolgellau it stood not on a timber pier but masonry footings and was filled from a pipe which tapped water from a stream on the hillside.

Photo: C.L.Caddy.

The last few miles of the journey, particularly between Penmaenpool and Arthog were on a stretch under threat from the tidal activities of the river (Afon Mawddach). Erosion was a constant menace which kept the civil engineer fully occupied. The four views on this page illustrate the nature of the coastline.

156. Penmaenpool. 31st May 1963. Minutes after leaving Penmaenpool, BR Standard Class 4MT 4-6-0 No.**75009** comes into close contact with the river with the 9.27am ex Ruabon train. The line would literally cling to the shore for the next couple of miles. *Photo: Peter E.Baughan.*

157.(Centre) **Arthog.** Relegated to a more mundane way of life, this former Cambrian stalwart, 2-4-0 moves forward towards Penmaenpool after having its loads of stone deposited on the shoreline.
Photo: Authors Collection.

158.(Bottom-left). Just a short distance east of the centre photograph, the sweeping reverse curves are highlighted. The stone off-loaded from the train is just visible in the middle right of the picture.
Photo: Authors Collection.

159. (Bottom-right). Fresh loads of ballast have been deposited, a requirement made necessary in exposed areas such as this where erosion problems were ever present. Note the encroaching waters to the left, giving that constant reminder of its presence.
PhotoL Authors Collection.

Penmaenpool boat disaster, 22nd July 1966. The 'Prince of Wales' is recovered prior to examination shortly after the accident. Much of the station (seen in the background) was still intact at this time. *D. J. Lowe Archive*

Penmaenpool boat disaster. The boat 'Prince of Wales' is recovered. Fifteen people including four children lost their lives here, when the ferry boat from Barmouth collided with the toll bridge on 22nd July 1966. A memorial service was conducted on the shoreline near the bridge in 2006 to mark the 40th Anniversary of this tragic happening. *D. J. Lowe Archive*

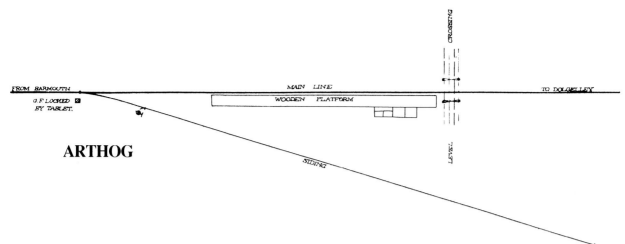

ARTHOG

PENMAENPOOL TO BARMOUTH JUNCTION

Apart from a short rise and fall after leaving Penmaenpool the line was level for the remaining four and three quarter miles to Barmouth Junction following the coastline for most of the way. The Electric Train Tablet section was from Penmaenpool to Barmouth Junction, with special provision built in for locomotives going on and off shed.

ARTHOG

Four miles from Penmaenpool, and an intermediate halt, Arthog consisted of a single wooden platform on the Down side of the line, with wooden buildings that housed a Booking Office, General Waiting Room, Ladies Waiting Room with Lavatory and a Gentlemens Lavatory. There was also another wooden hut that served as a Lamp Room. There was one siding also on the Down side which could hold 18 wagons, and was controlled by a 2 lever frame which was released by a key on the Electric Train Tablet. The staff consisted of a Class 6 Station Master and a porter, who also attended to the long burning lamps at Penmaenpool and Dolgellau. Goods traffic provided the bulk of the receipts in 1924.

160. Arthog. 31st May 1963.[Above] Viewed from a Barmouth bound train entering Arthog, note the Down siding which was controlled by a Ground Frame. The siding was closed to all traffic from 4th May 1964. The platform displays an elegant post and lamp casing housing a tall glass chimneyed lamp. *Photo: Peter E. Baughan.*

161. Arthog. 31st May 1963. At the turn of the century Solomon Andrews and Son of Cardiff unsuccessfully tried to develop the area around Arthog as a coastal resort. As it was, fame passed Arthog by and the isolated wooden station buildings look splendidly and decrepitly rural as the "Gents" subsides quietly on its brick foundations.
Photo: Peter E. Baughan.

Arthog Halt, looking towards Morfa Mawddach, (about three quarters of a mile away). Note the presence of the Camping Coach in the Down siding at this time, 31ˢᵗ August 1957. This Western Region facility was open to holiday makers (from 1953 to 1962), who would be encouraged to travel here by train and make use of the railway for visiting other holiday locations in the area. The Arthog Station Master would be on hand to provide local produce such as fresh milk, eggs and bread. The coach was removed from 1963 when the line came under LMR control. The siding was closed to all traffic from 4ᵗʰ May 1964.

D. J. Lowe Archive

BARMOUTH JUNCTION (until 1960)
MORFA MAWDDACH (from June 1960)

The Chester District Traffic Managers section ended at the Down distant signal for Barmouth Junction and control now passed to the Oswestry District Traffic Manager.

Originally the station was called Barmouth Ferry, until 1871 when the name was changed to Barmouth Junction, probably the name by which it was better known until June 1960 when it was changed to Morfa Mawddach. The station was set in isolated countryside with no houses and only a track across the dunes to connect it with the road. It was the creation of the line to Dolgellau that established the junction although it was not until the through route to Chester opened that saw it becoming established.

The station formed a triangular junction with the line from Barmouth meeting at the apex of the triangle with the Ruabon and Dovey Junction lines. The Chester line forked left, with its Up line platform exposed to the elements with only a small wooden shelter for protection. The Down Ruabon line was an island structure with the coast line to the south occupying the western face. The Down line from Dovey Junction also had a very basic shelter but with its back to the sea, similar to that on the Up Ruabon line. The island platform building was constructed of brick with a canopy extended part way over each platform face giving limited protection. At one time a Refreshment Room was operated, but this closed some time before the Dolgellau line services were withdrawn. A reversing line extended from the Down Ruabon line but outside the crossover to the commencement of the single line, and formed the third chord of the triangle. It connected with the extension of the Up main [coast] line after the crossover to the commencement of the single line. Coast line and Ruabon line freight trains transferred loads here rather than in Barmouth, and at one time there was accommodation available for storage of wagons but which were taken out some time before the line closed. The triangle was only used by locomotives from Ruabon, Portmadoc and Machynlleth which needing to turn prior to the

return working. One siding off the Down Ruabon line spur ran into a bay platform and before the war was used to park camping coaches. Passengers who changed here and needed to cross the tracks did so at the Barmouth end of the platform, over the barrow crossing, where they were under the eye of the signalmen in the box close by. The box itself was an all wood construction which housed a frame with a set of 38 levers. There was a walkway from the foot of the box to the centre of the coast line tracks where the signalman would exchange tokens with the footplate crew. At one time there were a couple of cottages near the Coast line, south of the platforms within the triangle, but these were removed some years ago. The points controlling the reversing line were hand operated. There was no provision for trains to work through from the Dolgellau line to the Dovey junction line, although there had been a proposal to extend the loops to enable this to be possible in the late 1930s.

BARMOUTH JUNCTION TO BARMOUTH

This section has been dealt with in some detail in the companion volume in the series. Once the single line section to Barmouth was regained the line ran along a low embankment before entering the 113 span viaduct. Sections of the bridge were rebuilt at differing times, with the main opening section, which was originally constructed as an overdraw type, being replaced by a swing opening structure. The bulk of the timber was of Baltic origin, delivered direct to the site and which withstood ravages of time until the early 1980s when a species of marine worm infested the structure, and which nearly closed the line. Fortunately, finance was made available to treat and restore the structure and the line once more carried locomotives and loco hauled stock, although such workings are confined to the summer months, the usual traffic being DMU workings. Nowadays, there is no regular freight traffic and even the signalmen have disappeared, being replaced by Radio controlled equipment.

162. Barmouth Junction. c.1960. An unusual wide-angle view of both road and rail approach to Barmouth Junction from Dolgellau. Although principally a rail interchange point without main road access, a track of sorts would appear to have existed, the GWR took over a roughly metalled by-way from the Cambrian Railways, and by the end of the B.R. era it had become the re-inforced concrete roadway of the photograph. It was adopted by the County Council in 1978. The site was used as the storage point for all the materials accumulated during the construction of the bridge, viaduct and accompanying works. Tramways were laid to bring in stone from local quarries. Eventually Solomon Andrews took over the disused tramways when they bought land, to the east of the site of the completed bridge, for prospective development.
Photo: Speed Publications.

BARMOUTH JUNCTION

c.1958

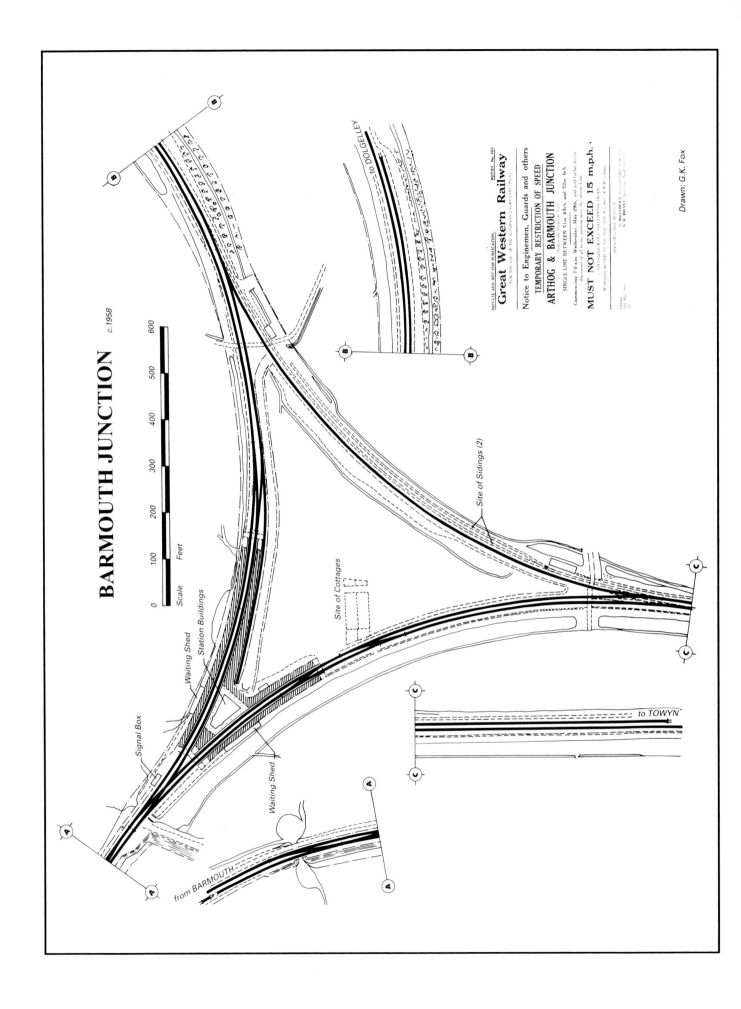

Scale Feet
0 100 200 300 400 500 600

Signal Box

Waiting Shed

Station Buildings

Waiting Shed

Site of Cottages

Site of Sidings (2)

from BARMOUTH

to TOWYN

to DOLGELLEY

Drawn: G.K. Fox

163. Barmouth Junction. An 'Aberdare' class outside framed 2-6-0 prepares to leave the single line section adjacent to the site of one of the three signal boxes which were present at Barmouth Junction until the early 1930's. Closure of the southern and eastern boxes also saw track layout alterations which simplified operations for working to and from the Ruabon line. This rationalization however put an end to through running from the Ruabon to the Coast line in an east/southern direction. In this view, the two lines in the foreground come together to form a headshunt alongside the Ruabon line.

Photo: Authors Collection.

164. Morfa Mawddach. 31st May 1963. 52m 17$\frac{1}{2}$ch have been traversed since B.R. Standard Class 4MT 4-6-0 No.**75009** passed Llangollen Line Junction with the 9.27am Ruabon to Barmouth stopping train, (7.50am Birkenhead to Pwllheli working, Reporting Number 2V89) which coasts past the Up branch lower quadrant signal (No.33) with its tubular post topped with a neat ball and spike finial and to arrive at Morfa Mawddach punctually at 12.00 noon. Notice the two bracket signals at the far end of the station, one for the line from Dolgellau, the other for the coast line from Towyn. Just visible by the smokebox is one of the three camping coaches resident at the station for the season.

Photo: Peter E. Baughan.

165. Morfa Mawddach. 31st May 1961. Mid-day at Morfa Mawddach, with 4-6-0 No.**75009** standing in the Down branch platform. Reading from left to right, the signals, seen above the fireman working on the tender of the locomotive are, 3. and 2. on the Down Main Line (from Towyn) and 5. and 6. on the Down Branch (Ruabon) line. In the middle distance the 11.00am from Machynlleth has just departed for Barmouth. On the left of the curve a yellow-painted fishtail warning board and a 10 m.p.h. temporary speed restriction sign. The token exchange apparatus is beside the wooden signal box. Two members of the Permanent Way staff are working by the fencing. Interestingly only the front windows of this Up branch shelter are fitted with security grilles whilst half round battens add extra security to the roof against the onslaught of high winds.

Photo: Peter E. Baughan.

166. Morfa Mawddach. 7th October 1960. 43xx Class 2-6-0 No.**6357** rests at Morfa Mawddach after working the 7.50am Birkenhead to Pwllheli (9.31am from Ruabon), awaiting termination of station duties, and for the Machynlleth to Barmouth train to leave ahead of us in order to clear the section. Fireman J.A. Jones of Chester takes a well earned rest on his rather uncomfortable tip-up seat whilst the duty porter unloads the crates of milk that have been put into the front van at Bontnewydd. They would be trundled along to No.3. Up Main platform for onward transmission. *Photo: Norman Jones.*

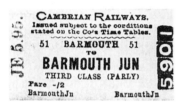

167. Morfa Mawddach. c.1963. On summer Saturdays, there was a considerable amount of light engine working at Morfa Mawddach, with locomotives working to and from Barmouth across the bridge, turning on the triangle which surrounded the station site. This meant that line occupation between the Junction and Barmouth South was more or less continuous during the day and signalmen were hard pressed to find paths for light engine movements. Additionally, where locomotives were required to undertake maintenance or disposal duties, or needed mechanical attention, it was necessary to travel to Penmaenpool, the nearest shed. Some early afternoon turns to Ruabon were worked by Penmaenpool shed who prepared their own engine and worked L.E. to Barmouth to pick up the stock. This may be the case with No.**75029** seen here entering/leaving the single line section to Penmaenpool. If the loco is working to Penmaenpool, why is it displaying the wrong headcode?
Photo: Authors Collection.

168. Morfa Mawddach. c.1963. B.R. Standard Class 4MT 4-6-0 No.**75021** of Croes Newydd shed (89B) enters Morfa Mawddach with a Barmouth to Ruabon train. The three coach formation was usual for a mid-week working, but in all probability extra coaches would have been added for a Saturday turn. Notice the signalman's walkway across the tracks - referred to in the text - the Setting Down Post with its bull's-eye lantern focussed on the catcher hook and the wooden stage to enable the signalman to reach up and lift the carrier down after the train had passed. On the extreme left are the usual "BEWARE OF TRAINS" notice, essential warning in view of the fact that the crossing was used by passengers, and the 20 m.p.h. speed restriction sign imposed over the entire length of the viaduct and bridge.
Photo: Authors Collection.

BARMOUTH

Until Nationalization, many of the passenger trains and all of the freight workings off the Ruabon line terminated at Barmouth although there was some increased through working in the summer months and particularly on Saturdays when seasonal holiday traffic from Butlins Camp at Penychain worked through to Birkenhead or Birmingham via Ruabon. Trains working forward over the route would have a change of crew here, and Penmaenpool, Bala or Croes Newydd men would take over and be relieved in their turn down the line. Frequently the trains would be double headed and there would be anxious moments to ensure that crew change over schedules were feasible and not disrupted. Locomotives that had worked up from Croes Newydd were required to be turned which meant that the 55ft. turntable in Barmouth yard was too small to accommodate the 43xx class 2-6-0s which performed the majority of work over the line. So, if they had worked to Barmouth with stock, this was disposed of and then the loco returned over the bridge when a path was available, where they would turn on the triangle and return back to Barmouth before awaiting their return working.

Quite often, relief sets would take over from Chester, Croes Newydd or Barmouth contemporaries who would have their break whilst the loco duties were attended to by Penmaenpool men. In times of extreme pressure, the locomotives going over the bridge to and from turning would be attached as pilot engines just to save time.

The local shuttle between Barmouth and Dolgellau was worked by an auto train set with Penmaenpool men, and until the final years, 0-6-0PT or 0-4-2Ts would work a single or sometimes with a double coach set when the service was well patronised. To save platform occupation, particularly on Saturdays, these local trips would start and finish from the excursion platform, located south of the level crossing, thus avoiding the need to open and close the gates. Latterly two non corridor coaches were used with an ex LMS design 2-6-0, probably 46446, 46516 or 46521, with the engine running around the stock at each end. The stock for the shuttle was parked at Dolgellau each evening, and the locomotive worked LE from and to Penmaenpool to take up the working.

169. Barmouth. c.1963.B.R. Standard Class 3MT 2-6-2T No.**82032** approaches the shortened Borthwen Viaduct after crossing the estuary with a Machynlleth to Pwllheli working. The last coach is crossing the lifeboat slipway. These engines were the first modern tank locomotives to appear on the former Cambrian and GWR lines and replaced the smaller B.R. Standard Class 2MT 78xxx series tender engines which were considered underpowered for some of the work. The 2-6-2T engines were popular with traincrews, but it was found that the water capacity was insufficient for some of the workings. Consequently some were transferred away, and were replaced by the 80xxx series Class 4MT 2-6-4T which were masters of the job, and which worked successfully until the withdrawal of steam in 1965. No. 82032 transferred to Bangor [6H] from where it was withdrawn in December 1965. The class rarely worked on the Ruabon to Barmouth line.
Photo: Authors Collection.

170. Barmouth. 7th August 1959. The large boiler and protruding smokebox accomodating the superheater header together with the large square boiler mountings invested Mr.C.B.Collett's 2251 Class of 0-6-0 with an agressive, thrusting appearance, personified by No.**3201** seen here leaving Barmouth with an "ordinary" passenger train comprised of a quite varied collection of coaching stock, including a S.R. Utility van. Observe the South signal box on the extreme left of the picture, on the right the excursion platform and (locked) wooden shelter, also the spiked iron railings of the perimeter fence. The locomotive carries an Croes Newydd (84J) shedplate which suggests that this working was to Ruabon. Several members the same class of engine were found on the coast line but they would have carried Machynlleth (89C) shedplates. The Oswestry and Chester Divisions kept their locomotive stock to their own lines wherever possible. *Photo: R.W.Hinton.*

171. Barmouth. c.1951. 58xx Class 0-4-2T No.**5808**, allocated to Kington near Leominster in December 1947 stands at the Up platform at Barmouth with a substantial load of assorted coaching stock for a Class 1P engine. The picture throws up several questions. There was little work for this class of engine at any of the Cambrian Coast sheds. It was not attached to Penmaenpool, the locomotive based there worked the auto-train shuttle between Dolgelley and Barmouth and had to be fitted for auto-train working and would have been in the 14xx series. There were two engines in the same series based at Bala, but Bala and Penmaenpool sheds came under Croes Newydd (84J) shed, so why is 5808 carrying a Machynlleth (89C) shedplate? What has happened to the cast smokebox numberplate? Finally, where is the head or tail lamp? Perhaps the driver could be traced and explain the mystery. *Photo: T.Lewis.*

172. Barmouth. 3rd. October 1964. This classic view of Barmouth in the final months of steam and also of the line from Morfa Mawddach to Ruabon. L.M.S. Standard Class 2MT 2-6-0 No.**46521**, nominally allocated to Machynlleth (6F) but based at Penmaenpool for working the Dolgellau to Barmouth local is seen here standing in the excursion platform, which was also used for the shuttle. With the withdrawal of auto-train operation it became necessary to use standard non-corridor coaching stock, the locomotive running around the stock at each trip. The local journeys were very well patronised and sorely missed by the local people when the line closed shortly after this view was taken.

Photo: M.Welch